PROTOTYPE AND DREAM CARS

PROTOTYPE

AND

DREAM CARS

DEWAR McLINTOCK

CHARTWELL
BOOKS, INC.

A QUINTET BOOK

Published by Chartwell Books
A Division of Book Sales, Inc.
110 Enterprise Avenue
Secaucus, New Jersey 07094

ISBN 1-55521-458-4

This book was designed and produced by
Quintet Publishing Limited
6 Blundell Street
London N7 9BH

Creative Director: Peter Bridgewater
Art Director: Ian Hunt
Designer: Nicki Simmonds
Artwork by Danny McBride
Project Editor: Shaun Barrington

Typeset in Great Britain by
Central Southern Typesetters, Eastbourne
Manufactured in Hong Kong by
Regent Publishing Services Limited
Printed in Hong Kong by
South Sea Int'l Press Ltd

CONTENTS

INTRODUCTION

TOP One of the prettiest cars of all time. The Chevrolet Corvette was born in 1953. Car shown is the 1963 Stingray with retractable headlamps.

ABOVE A somewhat surrealist version of the Chrysler Dart, by stylist and consultants Ghia of Turin; designed to shock, but the aerodynamics look questionable.

Much of this book is about cars you have never seen nor ever will see in the showrooms. It is about evolution, development, and trends, and about success and failure, past, present and future.

The term 'concept cars' has now universally come to mean designs which are so advanced as to be almost bizarre in some cases. Production may catch up with them quite quickly or very slowly. Usually they appear annually at the important motor shows at Geneva, Frankfurt, Paris, New York.

Prototypes are less idealistic and fantastic. Indeed, they are usually practical and realistic mock-ups or models upon which production cars are based. A small producer may need only a single prototype. A large mass producer may make a choice from dozens of prototypes, all differing in some way. Let loose on the roads for exhaustive testing, a prototype may be heavily disguised, to fool the competition, the media and the public. A large manufacturer may sometimes build several hundred pre-production cars, putting them in the hands of fleet owners or members of the public so that bugs can be ironed out.

Some hand-built cars and exotica are not so far removed from prototypes. If a small firm is making two or three cars a

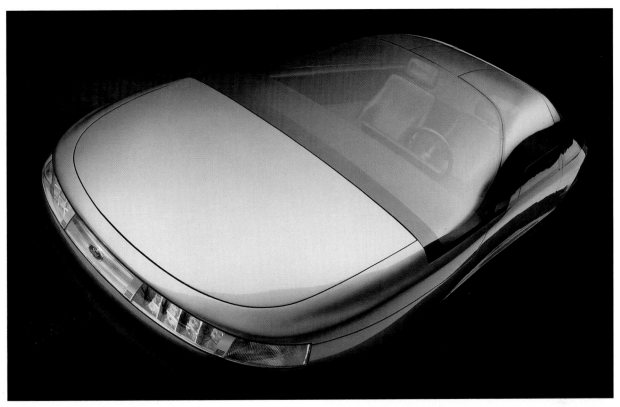

week, using a small labour force and relatively simple machinery, no two cars will be quite alike, or certainly not in the sense that modern quantity-produced cars are alike. The individuality of the hand-crafted car is, of course, what the customer pays so much for.

As to dream cars, the term is pretty well self-explanatory. Such cars have certainly come further than the drawing board or the design workshops. They are available – at a price – Such cars are examined in this book because they represent the *triumph* of the concept car and the prototype. They are the apogee of design and development: the seamless progress from inspiration to technological refinement and styling at its very best ends with them.

This book also includes significant material on the relationship between advanced cars and associated or independent mechanical systems and components, the widely applicable breakthroughs which sometimes come out of specific concept car problems. The whole subject is of course so vast that the choice of cars has to be limited. If anyone's favourite cause célèbre – or even lost cause – is absent from this work, it does not mean that it has been considered unworthy of attention.

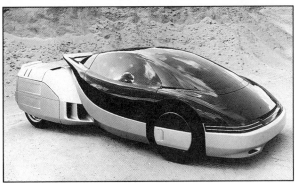

ABOVE The Alien, by the English design group IAD (International Automotive Design), first exhibited at the Turin Motor Show in 1986. The main concept behind the fibreglass mockup is the clear, visual division of the driving compartment from the running gear. 'A new aesthetic . . . for the sports car of the 1990s' said the company. Any takers? Not so far.

TOP Ford's Probe series of concept cars were futuristic but practicable. This is Probe V, with armoured plastic bubble top and multi-faceted headlamps.

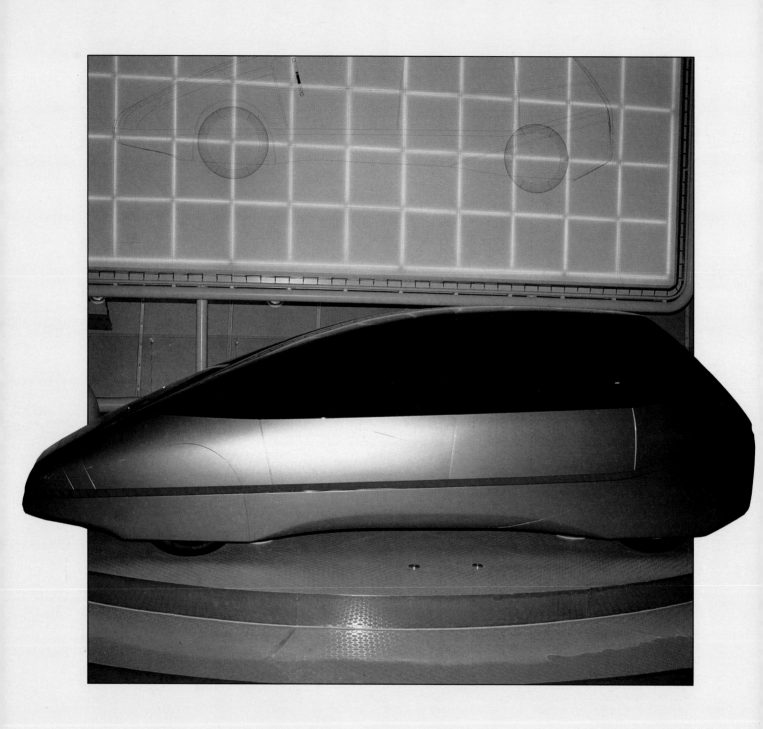

chapter one

CONCEPT CARS

This is just about as far as you can go in the concept car
business. It comes from the normally very conservative
BMW concern.

ABOVE Star attraction of the 1988 salons was the Jaguar XJ 220 – purely a concept car and funded quite meagrely, but wealthy potential buyers tried to put in orders.

All concept cars are exciting because, to the general public, they are unattainable; although this does not prevent people seeking them desperately. When Jaguar showed the V12 XJ 220 to an amazed showgoing public in 1988, people queued up to thrust in their cheques, which were promptly returned. The XJ 220 was, in any case, fairly far removed from reality – an ephemera in steel and aluminium with missile looks and awesome power, and a proposition very different from some concept cars which, via prototypes, turn quite quickly into production models, or which are mobile test beds for components and systems soon to be built into updated or completely new mass market cars.

Gestation period for the big cat was about three years, but some concept cars are born and weaned in months or even weeks. Swiss designer Franco Sbarro and his partner Dominique Mottas took only ten weeks to put together their 1989 concept car, with its startling hubless wheels and space-age monocoque. Sbarro said:

'Stylistically speaking, I work as a team with Camille Diebold on the basic sketches. I put across my ideas to him in the form of rough sketches, which he then repro-

duces in drawings and accurate illustrations that bring out the specific character of my bodywork designs. Sometimes we have a bit of fun making a 1/5 scale model that serves as a kind of dress rehearsal for the real thing.'

Continental European designers have always had a flair for futuristic concepts. Ghia – which nowadays also means Ford – recently created the Ghia Via as a realization of the sports car for the year 2000. It is not as wild as some concept cars and indeed no more bizarre than a production Ferrari Testarossa. 'The car's shape is dynamic yet the Via does not lose touch with reality' stated Ghia's Filippo Sapino, who heads the team at Ford's Turin design studio.

But the Via is rich in advanced features, such as an automatically adjusting rear spoiler, photosensitive glass roof with detachable targa, tiny ultra-powerful fibre-optic headlamps at the base of the windscreen and revolutionary fibre-optic instrumentation.

Dressing Up

Another twist to the 'concept concept' is to take a very ordinary existing production model and festoon it with new features, which is what Ford did with the Fiesta, in the form of the Urba city car.

It had a single door on the driver's side and two doors for the passengers. You could have it in any colour so long as it was bright yellow, for safety. There were electronic sensors in the bumpers, a thermostatic warm or cool food storage cupboard, a safety deposit box and an infra-red remote control lock/alarm system. Runflat tyres made a spare wheel superfluous. Always with such transformations there lurks the question – is this an advertising exercise or a real arts design?

Security is the keynote in a concept car developed by Austin Rover at the request of the Home Office in Britain, in support of the 1988 Conference on Crime Prevention. In this Rover Sterling various systems are incorporated, aimed at defeating the opportunist thief. The three main requirements are met: to prevent entry to the car, to make it protest loudly if its defences are breached, and to stop it being driven away.

ABOVE Ford make good use of Ghia, the Italian design outfit which it controls. Although a concept car, this sleek coupe could very easily be put into production.

TOP Rear-motored and 4WD, the MG EX-E concept car has a droop nose continuing the line of the bubble top. The top is ceramic-coated polycarbonate.

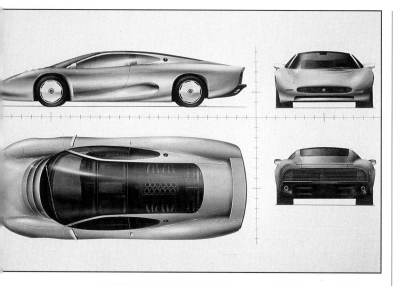

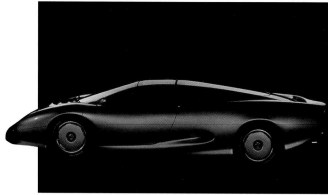

RIGHT The motor show crowds found the Jaguar XJ 220 quite breathtaking, the magic of the name being enough for some.

TOP From any angle, the XJ 220 looks beautiful and is aerodynamically immaculate. Wide tyres put plenty of rubber down.

ABOVE Contour-scooping of the sides of the Jaguar is aimed as much at motor cooling as at aerodynamic air flow.

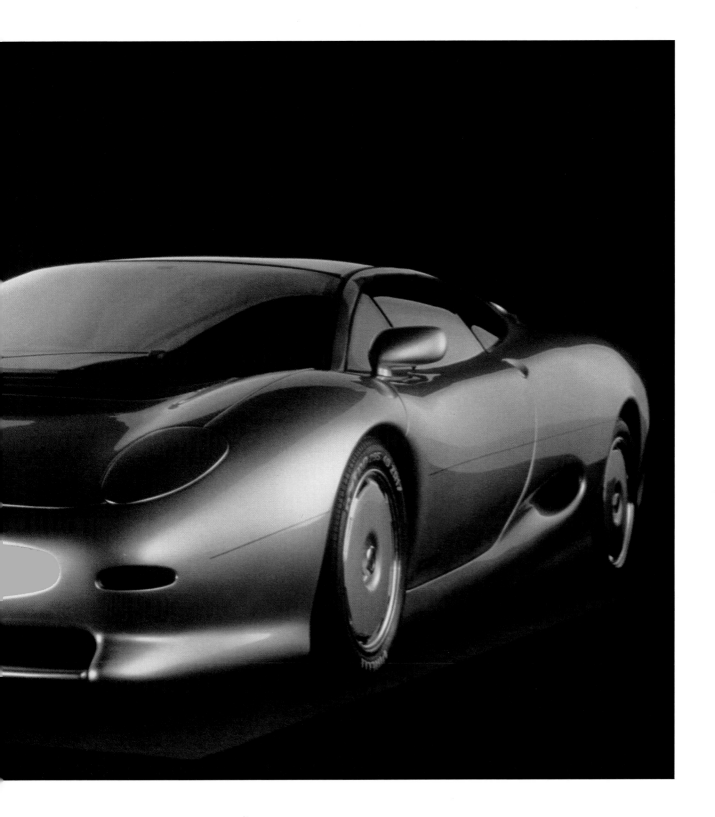

Rover's CCV (coupe concept vehicle) was not a model
intended for production, but more as a pointer to future
styling. The high-visibility roof is steel-supported.

But concept cars and prototypes have been thick on the ground with ARG (Austin Rover Group) in recent years. In 1985 the MG EX-E made its début (no closer now to actual production) and in 1986 came the Rover CCV (Coupé Concept Vehicle) which, unlike the MG, is not intended for production. Make-up of the CCV bodyshell is conventional but front and rear areas are designed to American standards with moulded impact absorbing structures. Drag coefficient was predicted at Cd. 0.27. A ceramic-coated polycarbonate roof panel incorporates a glass sunroof over a steel frame as used on the MG EX-E. Will any of these features make it onto the road?

Rover declare: 'This is a full four-seater, blending prestigious elements with the luxury of a high-quality sporting vehicle' – which can mean pretty well anything, but it is important that it is a four-seater.

The fascia takes the ergonomic lead as on the MG concept, with mini-binnacles on each side of the steering wheel, featuring, inter alia, suspension settings, spoiler adjustment and vehicle environment controls.

À La Mode

The French motor industry has always been very fecund in the creation of concept and protogenic cars, some of which, like the Renault BRV of 1974 and the Citroen Activa of 1988, quite quickly became the pre-production and eventually production models.

The BRV was a government-backed project aimed at the development of safer cars. The Régie insisted that it was neither a prototype nor a pre-production vehicle, nor even a styling exercise, least of all a dream car. Features of the BRV were progressively introduced in original or modified form into many future models, particularly the Renault 30.

In 1979 came the EPURE safety car (Étude de la Protection des Usagers de la Route et de l'Environment) based on the Renault 5 and the EVE economy car (Économie Vehicule

Cockpit of the MG EX-E, like that of the Rover CCV, is
highly ergonomic, with binnacles each side of the wheel.
Note the steel roof frame.

Éléments). Features of EPURE included energy-absorbing front
and rear ends, strengthened passenger compartment, improve-
ment of impact zones between vehicle and passengers and
roll-over members incorporated in the roof. Many of the lessons
of the EPURE were incorporated in the production models of
the early 1980s.

EVE was based on the R18 and achieved nearly 50% better
fuel consumption with a low-drag body boasting a coefficient
of Cd0.239, which was at that time 43% better than that of the
average European car. Renault passed the project over to the
French Energy Saving Agency in June 1981

A revolutionary Renault concept car is the Megane, which
looks very futuristic but is in reality a kind of rolling laboratory
for the development and evaluation of systems and products of
progressive components manufacturers, as well as of systems
and parts devised by the Régie's own teams.

It is an executive-size saloon with a V6 3-litre 250 bhp
turbocharged engine. The low-drag body with a coefficient of
Cd0.21 allows the beefy engine to propel it at 160mph/257kmh,
or even more if mid-range performance is sacrificed. The car
has sliding doors and window glass of a new type developed
by an outside supplier.

The running gear embodies such modern features as four-
wheel drive, four-wheel steering and computer-controlled suspension. A new transmission gives the option of automatic or
manual control.

Many of these systems were present on earlier prototypes
or concept cars but were combined for the first time in this
very workable mobile test bed. The Megane bristles with
advanced equipment: a VDU in the centre console acting as an
information centre for anything from mechanical or instrument
faults to navigational information and route-finding; electronically-controlled air conditioning; roof-fitted folding video
screens for rear seat passengers; conductive-film screen
heater.

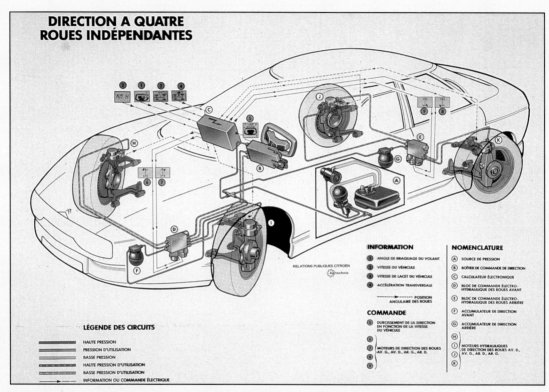

DIRECTION A QUATRE
ROUES INDÉPENDANTES

INFORMATION

① ANGLE DE BRAQUAGE DU VOLANT
② VITESSE DU VÉHICULE
③ VITESSE DE LACET DU VÉHICULE
④ ACCÉLÉRATION TRANSVERSALE

- - - - - → POSITION
ANGULAIRE DES ROUES

COMMANDE

⑤ DURCISSEMENT DE LA DIRECTION
EN FONCTION DE LA VITESSE
DU VÉHICULE

⑦ MOTEURS DE DIRECTION DES ROUES
AV. G., AV. D., AR. G., AR. D.

NOMENCLATURE

Ⓐ SOURCE DE PRESSION
Ⓑ BOÎTER DE COMMANDE DE DIRECTION
Ⓒ CALCULATEUR ÉLECTRONIQUE
Ⓓ BLOC DE COMMANDE ÉLECTRO-
HYDRAULIQUE DES ROUES AVANT
Ⓔ BLOC DE COMMANDE ÉLECTRO-
HYDRAULIQUE DES ROUES ARRIÈRE
Ⓕ ACCUMULATEUR DE DIRECTION
AVANT
Ⓖ ACCUMULATEUR DE DIRECTION
ARRIÈRE
Ⓗ
Ⓘ MOTEURS HYDRAULIQUES
DE DIRECTION DES ROUES AV. D.,
Ⓙ AV. G., AR. D., AR. G.
Ⓚ

RELATIONS PUBLIQUES CITROËN

LÉGENDE DES CIRCUITS

HAUTE PRESSION
PRESSION D'UTILISATION
BASSE PRESSION
HAUTE PRESSION D'UTILISATION
BASSE PRESSION D'UTILISATION
INFORMATION OU COMMANDE ÉLECTRIQUE

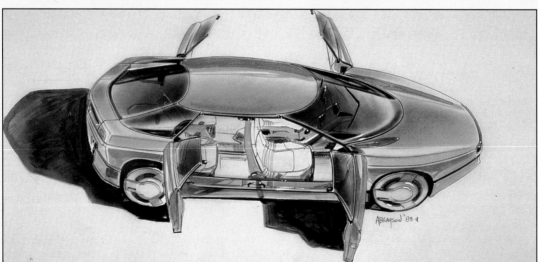

ABOVE One idea which the XM has not incorporated from the Activa is the door arrangement; for the XM, the doors are opposite-hinged.

TOP Citroen's Activa concept car of 1988. The illustration indicates features of the 'thinking' hydraulic suspension.

RIGHT The big, dramatically-sloped front and rear screens of the Activa give a near bubble-top effect; note the four-wheel steering.

ABOVE Renault described their Megane concept car as a
rolling laboratory for advanced features. The styling is
the almost mandatory wedge, droop nose, with 'slit-eye' headlamps.

LEFT The low-drag body of Megane has sliding doors.
Mechanicals include 250 bhp turbo motor, 4WD, 4WS,
computer-controlled suspension.

The Megane has not yet spawned any identifiable production
car, nor may it be intended as a pre-prototype, but Citroen's
Activa concept car, which first appeared at the Mondial de
l'Automobile, October 1988, has already been transmuted from
an ectoplasmic wonder into a very material member of the
Citroen family in the form of the XM top-of-the-range model,
which is already acclaimed as a new concept in executive cars.

Citroen claim that they created, for the first time in a series
production car, a 'thinking' hydraulic suspension system, combining the intelligence of electronics with the strength and
flexibility of hydraulics, the marriage of these two advanced
technologies having already been realized in the Activa project.
This advanced system, stated the firm, allied itself with front-
wheel drive, high-pressure braking with an anti-lock system,
and hydraulic steering assistance with variable speed-depen-
dent effort, to create an entirely new active-safety concept.

The Activa bore a remarkable resemblance visibly as well
as technically to the XM and one cannot help wondering if it
was not, in fact, a purely promotional exercise.

The styling of the XM was carried out with the help of
outside consultants and consumer clinics. Among the projects
presented, the one prepared by Bertone was accepted.

ABOVE Another styling exercise from the Citroen design department, the Karin, produced in 1980. A far less realistic design than the Xenia, such a slab-sided body shell would be extremely difficult to mass produce, and nothing ever came of it.

OPPOSITE The Peugeot Proxima is a spacious 2×2 concept coupé with a computer-controlled 600bhp V6 engine. It has ceramic lining on bearings and shafts and dry sump lubrication to reduce friction loss. 4WD is activated when sensors detect rear wheel spin. The twin turbos and fuel injection are also computer controlled. The clutch and gear box system is electronically controlled and has no mechanical linkage.

RIGHT 'Est-ce le break du futur?' Tomorrow's Estate perhaps? The Citroen Xenia is as yet no more than a scale model, but is a realistic approach to designing a sporty-looking 2×2 hatchback according to ergonomic principles. The interior includes some sophisticated technological features, such as microelectronic systems for all checks and solar cells to control air conditioning.

The British Bulldog

Aston Martin Lagonda is a kind of institution. Not given to the technical or promotional extravaganza, the firm tends to disclaim all knowledge of concept cars or even prototypes, but there was one occasion when enthusiasm overcame prudence and tradition. In 1979 Aston Martin's engineering department started on the detailed design work for a concept car, and the Bulldog was the result. Its name was the only thing traditional about it.

The idea for the car came during a lunchtime conversation between Michael Edwardes, then chairman of BL (British Leyland), and Alan Curtis, chairman of Astons. Perhaps the food was a little too good, but they found themselves talking quite seriously about an 'Aston–Jaguar' sports car. Curtis went back and commissioned designer William Towns to do some sketches. After a few minor setbacks, a car was built – in something like twelve months!

The 190mph/306kmh-plus Bulldog was only 3ft 7ins/110cms high, with angular lines and doors that had more of the bat

ABOVE With a mid-mounted motor, arrangements for cooling-air flow have to be carefully studied. Full air conditioning was a feature.

TOP Powerhouse of the Bulldog – a twin turbo Aston Martin V8 mounted amidships. It could squirt the car from 0 to 100mph in 10 seconds.

OPPOSITE 'Folded paper' styling and gull-wing doors were prominent features of the Aston Martin Bulldog of 1980. The car would do almost 200 mph.

than the gull about them. A twin-turbocharged V8 Aston Martin engine was mounted amidships. Five headlamps lay concealed behind a moveable flap and the instrumentation was digital.

The Aston wizards had been working on exhaust super-charging for a number of years, as had other manufacturers, and they were at least able to see their work realized in this unit with its twin Garrett blowers and Bosch mechanical fuel injection, although the firm was not yet ready for turbos.

The Bulldog could zap itself from zero to 60mph in 5 seconds and from zero to 100mph in 10 seconds. During early tests it lapped at more than 130mph/210kmh round a test track and later in the programme a speed of more than 170mph/274kmh was recorded.

Keith Martin, a member of the engineering team for the project, said the engine was based on the production V8 and had been able to take the extra power – about 60% more than the Aston Martin Vantage – without major modification, but

ABOVE Claimed as the most important newcomer in Aston Martin's 70-year history, the Virage. Power is from a 32-valve version of the all-alloy 5.4-litre V8.

TOP RIGHT A styling exercise by Ogle Engineering of Hertfordshire, England, the Aston Martin Ogle looked more Italianate than British, particularly at the rear end.

RIGHT Built for the Le Mans 24-hour race, the Nimrod Aston Martin. The relationship between production design innovation and racing is intimate and complex: those involved in racing will always claim that it is symbiotic and not parasitic, naturally enough.

the high-duty ZF gearbox was the only one available to take that amount of muscle.

At the time, Curtis said of the car: 'It is essentially an exercise to show that Aston Martin can build the ultimate road-going supercar. It will be for sale at the right price but was not built with selling in mind.

Corvette Indy

The mid-engined Chevrolet Corvette Indy concept car, first shown to the public in January 1986, was a work-in-progress report on the long line of Corvette research cars. Chevrolet's chief engineer, Don Runkle, said: 'We do these cars as much for inspiration as experiment, because it gives our people a chance to turn their dreams into reality.'

Corvette concept car No 1, back in 1959, was a small single seater designed to evaluate supercharging, fuel-injection systems and high-speed handling. CERV 1, as it was called, could do over 200mph/320kmh. The engine was mid-mounted.

CERV 2, in 1964, was also mid-engined. A two-seater, it was the first mid-engined car to have permanent four-wheel drive. Another mid-motor Corvette was the Astro II, of 1968 and this was followed by the XP-882 with a V8 motor mounted transversely between the rear wheels. Wankel rotary engine development made news in 1973 when Chevrolet showed two mid-motor rotary Corvettes, and in 1977 came the four-rotor Aerovette gull-wing roadster.

ABOVE 1964 Cerv 2, a mobile testbed from Corvette – and also an excuse for keeping Corvette on the track at a time when racing was frowned upon by the management.

TOP Features of the Corvette Indy of 1986 included 4WD, 4WS, ABS, traction control and active suspension. VDUs provided rear vision, navigation and performance information.

OPPOSITE Plump but suave, the Chevvy Corvette Indy of 1988 was so-called because it housed the Indianapolis V8 racecar motor with twin turbos.

ABOVE Seductive hi-tech cockpit of the '86 Indy.

The Indy, so called because it was engined with a version of the Chevvy Indy V8 racecar unit, was the basis for a running prototype with all-wheel drive, all-wheel steering, anti-lock braking, traction control and active suspension – the kind of technology that is in the air for tomorrow's production cars. The Indy's 2.65 motor has twin turbochargers and is multi-port fuel-injected.

A cathode ray tube on the fascia provides rear vision via a dedicated camera. Two other c.r.t. screens, one in each door, deliver information on vehicle dynamics, navigation and engine operation on command. Each door also houses individual climate and radio controls.

The computer-controlled wheel control system employs a sensor to read the accelerator pedal position and feed-back to the accelerator is via an electric motor. The system electronically limits wheelspin. The same sensors that read wheel lock-up in braking also send information to the wheel control computer when the car is accelerating.

Response of wheels and suspension is optimized electronically for all conditons, maintaining ride quality without compromising handling. Input from the wheel control system computer can alter suspension compliance instantly to absorb bumps or stiffen it for hard cornering.

ABOVE AND ABOVE LEFT Three concept cars from
Corvette that basically led nowhere: Astro I (above left),
Astro II (top), and Astro III (above). If you're searching for
genuine innovation, you can't win 'em all.

Getting Real

So many concept cars are so tenuously engaged in the realities of day-by-day transportation that it is quite refreshing to come upon the concept of a robustly realistic small utility car, like the Opel Junior of 1983.

The little car was rich in slightly off-the-wall ideas such as seat upholstery that could be removed and used for camping and a lockable fascia bar that could hold the usual instruments and accessory modules and could be removed for exterior use. Extra modules or gadgets could be added easily.

The Opel Junior had a drag coefficient of Cd0.31, which was creditable for a car with an overall length of only 11ft/3.35m. With its transverse-mounted 1.2 litre engine it would accelerate from 0 to 60mph in under 15secs and reach a top speed of 93mph/149kmh, according to engineering calculations. The car was built to aid the compilation of market research data on sales trends in European small cars at the start of the 1990s.

There was a choice of three roofs. The standard version – a two-piece detachable plastic unit – could be exchanged for a folding canvas top or a panoramic glass roof. The rear hatch was split into two parts at the waistline, the lower part folding upwards. There was all kinds of provision for luggage and oddments stowage. Vauxhall/Opel also had plans for a four-wheel-drive version with variable ground clearance. The car was not, of course, intended for production, but it would not be a difficult car to manufacture, using Nova components. The Citroen 2CV, Renault 4 and Fiat Panda all went into production very quickly after initial studies indicated that there was a market.

In 1987, Daihatsu came up with a mid-engined concept car which they called the Urban Buggy, and which, if produced, they claimed would be able to cope with conditions from 'comfortable high-speed cruising to rugged off-road exploring'. Power unit was that of the Charade GTi – a 1-litre turbo 3-cyl. The vehicle had a short, box-like body on a long wheelbase chassis with large tyres.

Features of the interior included a washable boat-deck type of floor, and sports-style front seats with full harness belts to hold driver and passenger safely in off-road driving. Front screen and rear window could be opened. Ford have also conceived a city car version of the new Fiesta, a notable feature of which is sensors in the bumpers, to help to avoid minor collisions.

The Nissan Jura has 4 wheel steering, full-time 4 wheel drive with electronic control, and electric sliding doors.

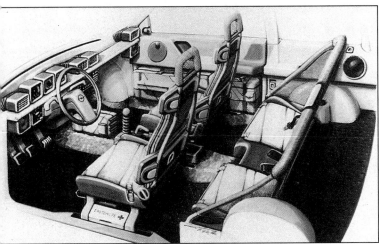

TOP A robustly realistic small car – the Opel Junior of 1983, built to aid market research on small utility cars.

ABOVE Removable seats and accessory modules gave adaptability to the Opel Junior. There were plans for a 4WD version.

The Vauxhall SRV of 1975 was a styling exercise – a crystallization of the lively and esoteric ideas of the firm's styling team headed by Wayne Cherry, an Anglophile American. But it was a study involving function as well as form, although there was no intention to put the car into production.

This was a 4-door coupé, only 41½in/105cm high, envisaged as a high-performance machine with a transverse motor boosted by an exhaust turbine mounted behind the passenger area. All four passengers and the engine were within the wheelbase. The front seats were fixed, but control pedals, steering column and front-seat rake were adjustable. Fixed front seats contributed to the overall strength of the body-chassis frame, which surrounded the passenger compartment.

Design concepts included trimming the car at high speed by the use of an aerofoil in the nose; incorporating an electric levelling system at the rear; and introducing aircraft technology by incorporating a pump system to vary distribution of fuel among the various tanks.

All control switches were mounted in the driver's door and grouped as in an aircraft cockpit. The instrument panel was mounted slightly to the side of the driver and swung outward

TOP Chubby frontal aspect of the Opel Junior
shows the wide tyres and clean design of light units.

BOTTOM Fenders of the little runabout are
cleanly contoured in tough plastic.

Well-established British design consultants and
manufacturers IAD were responsible for this unusual
concept, designated Impact.

as the door opened, to facilitate entry and exit. The pillarless body was of moulded glass fibre reinforced with carbon fibre to give strength to the resin – a technique which was gaining popularity. Tubular struts were used round engine and suspension mounts. The roof rails from screen to rear quarters served as roll-bars. Seats were set in deep-moulded recesses and seatbelts concealed in the frame and roof when not in use.

Hatches provided access to the engine compartment, rear axle and wheels. The tapered rear end housed the radiator, spare wheel and certain electrical equipment. Main forward lighting comprised Cibié iodine vapour headlamps, retracting when not in use. They revolved around their vertical axis, thus ensuring that there was no danger of their being improperly aligned vertically when brought into service.

TOP Based on the Ford Escort XR3, the Ghia Brezza takes coupe format. The almost totally covered rear wheel is unusual today.

ABOVE Somehow four people could cram into the Vauxhall SRV (Styling Research Vehicle). The car has a rear-mounted engine, and is only 41½ ins high.

High Speed Research

Mitsubishi's HSR (High Speed Research) car, introduced a few years ago, was notable in having such a low drag factor – Cd0.20 – that very high speeds could be expected without any more muscular an engine than a 16-valve 2-litre turbo, which would also be very economical. Turbo boost could be controlled either manually or by the on-board computer, to get either maximum acceleration or high-speed cruising with minimal fuel consumption. The HSR is of hybrid construction. The floor and sub-structure are a steel monocoque and the upper part of the cabin is a tubular steel framework, whilst the panelling is in composite Kevlar and polycarbonate materials, which are strong, light and easy to mould.

To make it easy to get into and out of the car, there is what Mitsubishi called an Integral Entry and Exit System. The seat slides sideways and is interlocked with the door. When the door is opened, the seat swings out with it and when it is shut, the seat automatically slots the driver into position behind the wheel. Permanent 4WD and 4-wheel steering are features of

the HSR and the conventional anti-lock braking system is backed up by race-derived air braking. The front and rear spoilers or wings are angled automatically when braking from high speed, to interrupt the air flow, creating extra drag and downforce.

Take your seat in the car and you seem to be projected a decade ahead. The main feature is a computer-controlled support system for the driver, which analyzes traffic information and external conditons such as changes in road surface, temperature, the strength of head and side winds and even the distance to the car ahead.

Laser-radar, a rear-view camera, forward-facing camera and a night vision camera for fast and safe night-time driving all relay information to the driver on a large display panel. The HSR also incorporates a navigation system which will direct the driver. With its optical fibre gyro system the car will check its relative location and by receiving traffic information will initiate route changes to meet the situation.

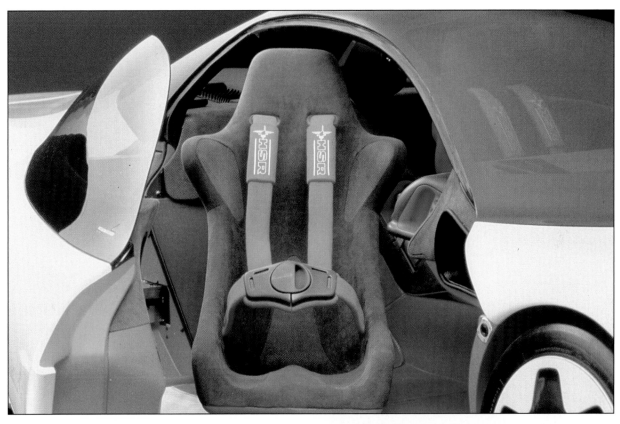

Silicone Implants

If a big corporation wants to have fun as well as serious and sometimes destructive testing of automotive components, there is no better way than taking to the race track. This is what is being done by General Electric Silicones with their SCCA (Sports Car Club of America) race car – a test bed for advanced materials and components concepts in the silicones field.

The SCCA class of sportster was chosen because it has a fairly conventional mid-engine format. With this arrangement, test results can be obtained very quickly and the results can be applied to prototypes or production vehicles.

In the important area of heat management, the GE race car has silicone-based coolant hoses and silicone foam heat shields on the firewall and inside the motor cowling. The car's rear universal joints are protected by silicone rubber boots and the exhaust system is coated with a high temperature-resistant silicone resin to give corrosion protection as well as to aid the retention of appearance.

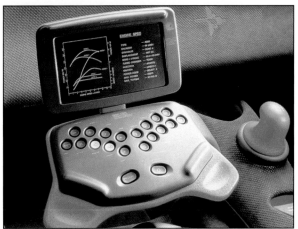

ABOVE Display panel of the HSR seems to tell the driver everything except his blood group.

TOP The integral entry/exit system makes every kind of sense, but harness-type restraint is controversial.

Existing electronics are simple, but there are plans for advanced concept development work in electronic controls for suspension and traction. Evaluation work in this area will centre on silicone coating systems and silicone copolymers for insulation.

Copolymer developments will probably also include the development of innovative silicone-organic copolymers and elastomers to enhance the qualities of conventional silicones with better abrasion resistance and fuel resistance.

According to GE Silicones, developments may well apply to such applications as drive belts, camshaft belts, engine mountings and isolators, suspension bushes and steering rack and pinion boots and gaiters.

Nissan's Cluster of Concepts

Nissan's second generation MID4 concept/prototype has been designed to deliver dynamic performance appropriate to a world-class sports car. The engine is a 3-litre V6 twin turbo of 330hp, longitudinally mounted amidships. The car has full-time 4WD with viscous differentials front, centre and rear. Anti-lock braking is naturally a feature.

As in most concepts, the shell is utterly smooth and the fenders are integrated. Large quanities of aluminium are used, with a weight saving of 25% compared with a steel body. Front suspension is double wishbone. The multi-link rear suspension is the same as that on the same firm's ARC-X concept car.

The ARC-X is a compact saloon which is virtually a mobile test shop for the popular modern technological 'intelligent' vehicle control components, in an integrated system. This implies automatic control of such functions as engine and transmission performance, steering, braking, suspension and air conditioning. The engine of the ARC-X is a 3-litre V6 quad-cam unit, mounted transversely at the front.

The Judo was developed as a recreational vehicle or urban 4WD runabout, with the following characteristics: generous performance for city and highway; rough-road capability; a comfortable, spacious cabin. Large-size dual-purpose tyres, a large skid-plate and the design of the rear spare wheel hanger 'create a wild 4WD image' as Nissan put it. Cabin equipment is 'designed to impress the sporty-minded'. The car has a full-length power sunroof, power spare wheel hanger and fold-away electric winch.

LEFT Sheer enjoyment, preferably in the sun, is the aim of the Nissan Saurus – a lightweight open two-seater with a dune buggy flavour.

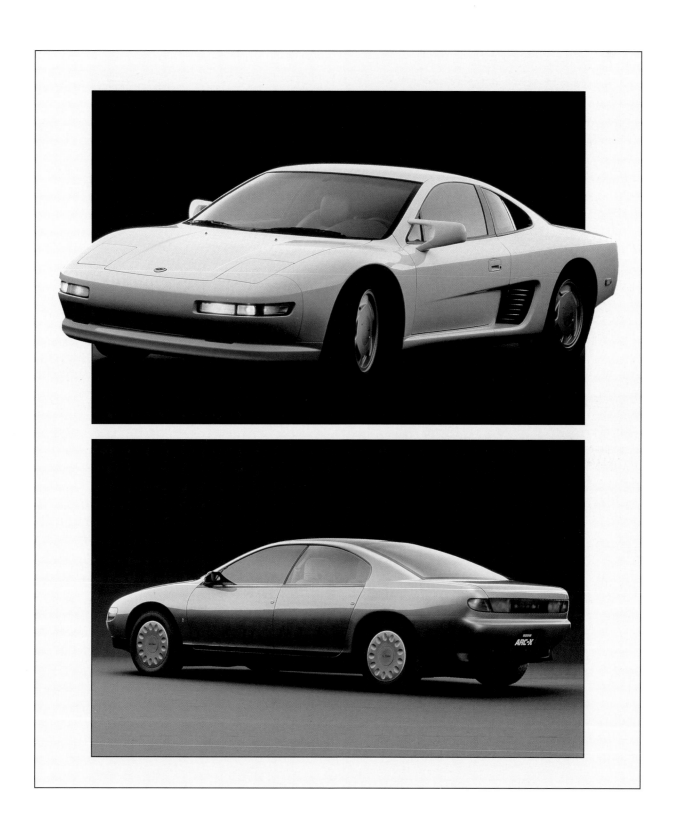

The Jura and Saurus concept cars were designed as a pair of vehicles with the respective roles of 'work tool' and 'pleasure device', following a way of thinking that is totally different from the conventional concept of multiple ownership. The Jura is a forward-control type of sedan with emphasis on its function as a work tool. Body contours are rounded and smooth and the wheelbase is long. There is an electric sliding side door with a broad sweeping curvature. Rear overhang is minimal and four-wheel steering is a feature, while the electronically controlled automatic transmission is as on the ARC-X. The full-time 4WD has a viscous differential. In the case of the Saurus, emphasis is on the 'pleasure device' side of the car's twin aspects. Nissan describe it as a new generation lightweight mid-engined sporting open 2-seater. A low, slim body

and large protruding tyres create a racing car image. The engine is supercharged and drives the rear wheels. 'The design concept was for a lightweight feel to allow the easy enjoyment of the sense of unity among man, machine and the wind,' explain the marketing men at Nissan, inscrutably.

ABOVE Nissan Judo is made for go-anywhere fun and capability, without sacrificing comfort and convenience.

OPPOSITE TOP Sleek concept/prototype MID 4 from Nissan – a sports supercar with 330bhp.

OPPOSITE BOTTOM Smart saloon amd mobile test shop, the Nissan ARC-X is packed with technological features.

chapter two

PROTOTYPES AND PRE-PRODUCTION CARS

From 1974 – a typical Pininfarina design, based on a
Ferrari coupe.

ABOVE The immortal Model T Ford in open tourer form. More than 16 million were made between 1908 and 1927.

RIGHT The Ford Probe V has a drag coefficient of 0.137, making it more aerodynamic than an F15 supersonic jet fighter. Gull-wing doors are a feature.

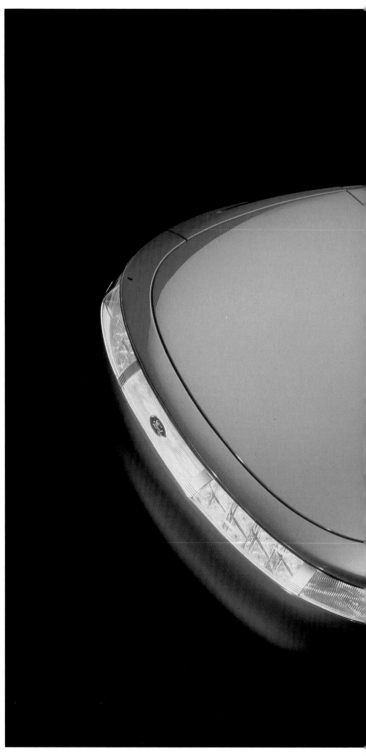

The first horseless carriages were at once both more and less than prototypes. Perhaps they were really concept cars . . . They were built in backyards and usually finished up on the roads for years or decades. Many of them are still around and in use, after almost a century. If a man built a car in those far-off days, it was a prototype but also often the first of the production cars, assuming he was going to make more than one. No sooner had he finished it than someone wanted to buy it.

Starting, rolling, stopping and steering. Those were the qualities that concerned the engineer in the beginning (and still do). They were the factors that not only filled the minds of the men on the mechanical side of design, but also influenced the stylists and body designers. You can't design a car simply by making pretty pictures and scale models, then putting in an engine and setting up a production line.

Design consists basically of mechanical and body engineering, with styling usually coming in at a later stage. You have a dialogue between the engineer and the artist, except in the rare cases where, initially at any rate, one man conceives a complete idea, as was the case with Henry Ford and the Model T, or Issigonis and the Mini. Sooner or later you need a team, even if the original idea is that of a single genius.

ABOVE The Turin designer Pininfarina not only restyled and converted standard models, but also built concepts and exotica such as this mid-engined sportster – the Modula.

LEFT Wrap-over sliding doors are a feature of Ford's Probe V. Body shell is a lightweight thermoplastic skin over a space frame.

The history of the construction of prototypes is a long one – as long, if you like, as that of the motorcar itself – but for our purposes we may feel that it should date from the start of quantity production or even mass production with its inevitable element of mechanization. And who started or 'invented' mass production of cars? Arguably it was Henry Ford, with the immortal Model T in 1908.

If you say 'Ford' it is like saying 'chair' or 'tree' or 'house'. It is a generic term – a phenomenon, an institution, and everyone in the world has heard of it. There must have been a few thousand Ford prototypes in nearly a hundred years, but the spindly object that started it all was the mock-up or buck for the Model T, assuming that Ford's original quadricycle of 1896 was a 'production car' (it sold for 200 dollars). From the mass production era onwards to today and into the indefinite future, prototypes are *de rigueur*; at first they were simply experimental full-size cars hand-built from full-scale working drawings. Frequently they used bought-in parts from component manufacturers – wheels, springs, sometimes even chassis members.

Quite soon, the techniques of creating visuals and making small-scale drawings and models came into favour and at the same time came the now-familiar mock-ups – the full-size models in materials such as wood, plastic, or plaster. The processes became much more complicated with the advent of the pressed-steel body in the early 1920s, while another revolutionary epoch in the story of auto production was the introduction of computer-aided design in the early 1960s.

The decade 1950–1960 was a watershed in which the individual designer was giving way to the small and then the large design team or department. Alex Issigonis, with his cigarette-packet sketches, eye for style and remarkable ability with hand and machine tools, was perhaps the last of the great individualists, although of course it took quite a few mock-ups and prototypes to get the Mini on to the production lines. But the point is that Issigonis could have made a perfectly feasible prototype with his own hands. (He had built and raced small cars with outstanding success.)

Teamwork and Freelancers

Issigonis always maintained that he was an engineer and not a stylist, but the same might have been said of the Pininfarina family of Italy, whose talents were also employed by the British Motor Corporation. It was a time when the motor industry

Styling detail of BMW M1 prototype. The turbocharged
M1 was a 3½-litre car and the basis for a Group 4 racer in
the early 1970s.

was starting to use specialist styling and design concerns in addition to their own design departments, and they usually had a favourite to whom they were loyal. For example, over the years General Motors commissioned many prototypes but only one outside supplier was ever considered for this work – that was Pininfarina. The sharp-edged look first introduced on the Cadillac Seville in 1976 and then on the more compact cars in 1977 is directly attributable to Pininfarina designs.

An example of today's weighty and costly design staffing and equipment is provided by the case of the little Citroen AX car, the gestation of which involved an average of 28 engineers, technicians and draughtsmen in 250,000 man-hours of study in a 3½-year period, plus 3,500 hours of computer time for structural optimization and 30,000 hours of laboratory testing. Even more time and effort might have been required had not the firm been able to draw on features and characteristics of its ECO 2000 concept car.

The AX was a very different story from that historic umbrella on wheels – Citroen's 2CV. It was conceived in 1935 when there wasn't a computer in sight and the first example was practically stapled together like a fruit box. Even so, over 200 prototypes were built, although all but two were destroyed when the Germans invaded. The project went underground with the pair of survivors. Forty-five years later, seven milion have been built . . .

A veritable legion of 'freelance' stylists and designers grew up around Turin and Milan, the focal centres of the Italian motor industry. The names of Pininfarina, Giugiaro, Bertone, Ghia, Zagato and Michelotti echo through the years and their work is as prestigious as that of the great couturiers. Their 'catwalks' are the stands at the international motor exhibitions. As well as designing new models, some of these specialists have production lines. Bertone, for example, manufacture the Volvo sports coupé, which is the Swedish company's prestige model in the USA. Pininfarina make most of the Ferrari bodies, as well as the nostalgic and coveted Alfa Romeo Spider. Pininfarina also have strong links with Honda and Peugeot.

ABOVE Wire wheels with centre-lock hubs were de rigeur for sports cars in the day of the SS 100. Running boards were still in fashion.

RIGHT A most imposing car, the SS 100 today commands fabulous prices but cost only £400 in 1936. Under the long hood was a 2½ or 3½-litre engine of Jaguar design.

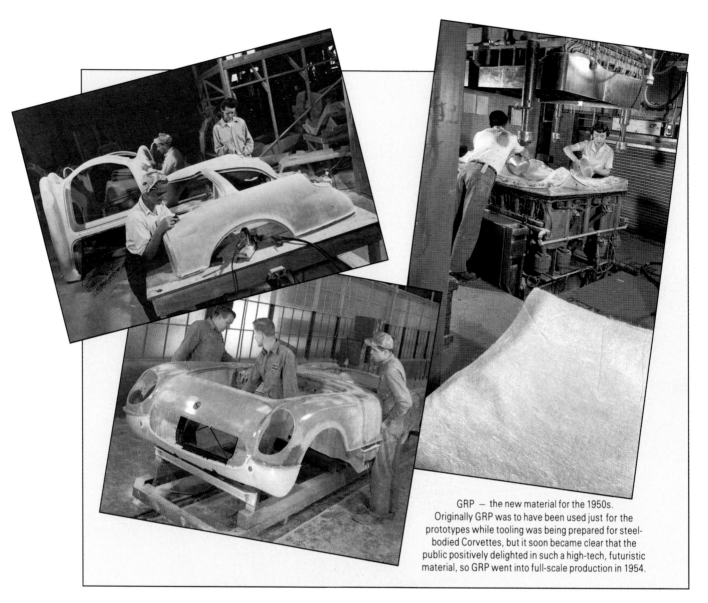

GRP — the new material for the 1950s.
Originally GRP was to have been used just for the
prototypes while tooling was being prepared for steel-
bodied Corvettes, but it soon became clear that the
public positively delighted in such a high-tech, futuristic
material, so GRP went into full-scale production in 1954.

Corvette

One of the prettiest of all cars, the Corvette was the brainchild
of chief engineer Ed. N. Cole and Harley Earl, who by 1950
were convinced that the firm needed a sporty roadster to meet
demand in a youthful and well-heeled sector of the market. It
was exhibited as a proto-concept car in 1953 and went into
pre-production soon after. It was unique in being one of the
first plastic-bodied cars to go into quantity production. The
prototypes used the recently established hand lay-up process
of panel construction, but more sophisticated moulding methods
were used in production. Throughout the motor industry, glass
and resin (glass fibre) techniques were proving useful not only
in prototype construction, but for production panelling in both
low- and high-production companies (albeit usually for
specialized models, and particularly sports cars).

Prototypes for the Chevrolet Corvette, which General Motors
called 'America's only authentic sports car' were comparatively
easy to create, once the stylists and draughtsmen had done
their work, because the design was based more or less on
stock mechanicals, and from the start the bodies were hand
laid-up in glass-reinforced resin construction. The first pre-
production car was built at Flint, Michigan, on June 30, 1953.

Originally a General Motors Motorama 'dream car', the
Corvette went into production after rave receptions on the
motor show circuit and has come to be one of the world's best

Probably America's most successful sports car, the Chevrolet Corvette (foreground) was created in 1953. Corvair and Nimrod, also seen here, were Chevvy sportsters that never made it into the big time.

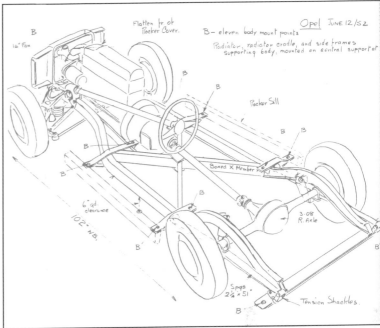

ABOVE Maurice Olley's original sketch for the top secret Opel, which would become the Corvette, turned out to be remarkably close to the eventual production frame.

LEFT By the late 1970s, Chevrolet Corvette contours had become slightly more flamboyant. Half a million 'Vettes had been built. This model is the experimental Turbo 'Vette 3.

known automobiles and the forerunner of numerous design advances in American cars. Over the years that followed, the Corvette's shape was considerably altered. Perhaps the Corvette Stingray of 1965 was the most attractive, although the earlier cars are more collectable.

In the mid-1970s a remarkable Corvette prototype took the form of a beautifully styled mid-engined car. This was Chevrolet's only flirtation with the Wankel rotary engine, which was up for grabs and infatuating several important manufacturers at the time. As is well known, Mazda has been the only firm to take it seriously, and very successfully so.

Glass fibre can be moulded to give more alluring curves than steel or aluminium, but there is a danger of overdoing it and coming up with baroque shapes. Alfa Romeo recently exhibited a positively vulgar-looking concept for a limited edition of 75 in resin-glass. The saving grace is a very low aerodynamic coefficient. It is to be built by Zagato and will be called Il Mostro – the Monster . . .

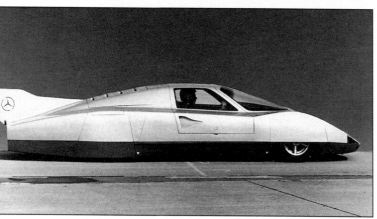

ABOVE The Mercedes-Benz C III-III was a test vehicle for diesel motors and for extreme aerodynamics.

TOP Captivating sports/racer – the Mercedes-Benz 300 SLR, which carried the German banner in the early 1950s.

Mercedes-Benz

One of the most beautiful cars ever to be built was the Mercedes-Benz 300 SL and it's fair to say that the prototype was the firm's handbuilt car with which it returned to racing in 1952, although there were numerous interim prototypes and pre-production cars. By 1954, after resounding sport-racing successes, Mercedes at any rate had on their hands at least one prototype that could be the model for almost instant production, although they tended to regard it as a concept car or a subject for the catwalk, to drum up publicity for the marque. In fact it was a sensation at the New York show. To quote the late Dennis May, a celebrated motor writer: 'There the matter might have rested if Max Hoffman, the US eastern seaboard's leading importer of European cars, hadn't enfiladed Stuttgart with demands for a catalogued, off-the-peg rendering of the New York show-stopper. These pleas prevailed and later in 1954 the die was cast. The gullwing coupé 300 SL, a thing of abiding beauty and an inflator of owners' egos, hit the

world's markets.' The car was the first production car to have petrol injection. Only 1400 were made.

A dramatic and technically interesting Mercedes prototype was the C 111 of 1969. This sports coupé also had gull-wing doors while its most interesting mechanical feature was the use of a rotary engine. But it never reached the production line. This preoccupation with gull-wing doors was no pretentious eccentricity. It is simply that if you base a car on a multi-tube space frame like a wine-basket, there's no place for ordinary doors. It always has to be remembered that invisible yet sub-stantial *people* have to be built into a prototype. The Japanese went wrong in the early days when they built prototypes and production cars round small men and women. Now the emphasis is all on spacious interiors, hence Fiat's ad: 'When we designed the Tipo we started at the bottom'.

That early 300 was superseded by much more restrained and less exciting roadsters, but today there is a very important new 300 SL series, in convertible form with an ingenious 'thinking' roll-over bar.

Like most cars of recent years, the 300 has a very low drag coefficient. It is what the engineer calls a very slippery car. Minimal air resistance means better performance and economy, and probably, although not necessarily, better looks. Drag reduction was largely guesswork or inspiration in earlier days, but the introduction of the wind tunnel revolutionized the whole business of shell design, for the companies who could obtain the use of one or who could have their own. Small producers sometimes construct small wind tunnels to take scale models.

ABOVE The charismatic 300 SL Gullwing, which now commands astronomical auction prices. The first production car with fuel injection, it started out as a concept car, but the US salesmen wanted the real thing. They got it: but only 1400 were made.

OVERLEAF The latest Mercedes SL series has a restrained yet quite modernistic appearance and includes many advanced features, such as a roll-over bar that locks in place in a fraction of a second on impact.

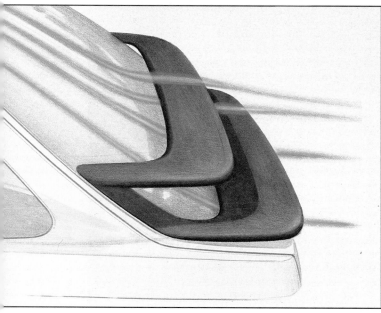

ABOVE Ford's early XR4 Sierra cars had this type of dual rear spoiler, developed in the wind tunnel during probe project research.

TOP Early model of Citroen concept design ECO 2000, as it would perform in the wind tunnel.

OPPOSITE Determining the aerodynamics of an Alfa Romeo 33 Giardinetta in the wind tunnel, using computer-generated isopressure maps

CADCAM

The technical equipment of a wind tunnel not only allows for aerodynamics research to be carried out, but makes it possible for all basic functional characteristics resulting from the flow of air round a vehicle to be measured. All the tests can be carried out under simulated natural conditions, from blizzard to tropical storm. The evaluation of air conditioning units and heating/ventilating systems can be done with the appropriate engine loadings by the simulation of rolling and climbing resistance and of air and acceleration resistance on the associated roller test bed. Such methods can minimize the necessity for teams of drivers to test cars intensively on and off roads in all kinds of conditions, although such evaluation will never be entirely eliminated.

In America and Europe in the 1970s manufacturers in the big league started to take advantage of what is known as CADCAM – Computer Aided Design/Computer Aided Manufacture. A strong interest in aerodynamics had of course arisen from the fuel crisis in the early years of the decade. It outlined the need for more slippery body shells for efficient air penetration. Wind tunnels and computerized design and manufacture supplied the answers. The CAD part of CADCAM allowed smaller tolerances on exterior structural details such as seams and welds, door shut lines, bumper shapes etc. CAM translated the information into engineering terms. CADCAM linked design and prototype teams to engineering teams electronically. The robots on the production lines were waiting to be fed . . .

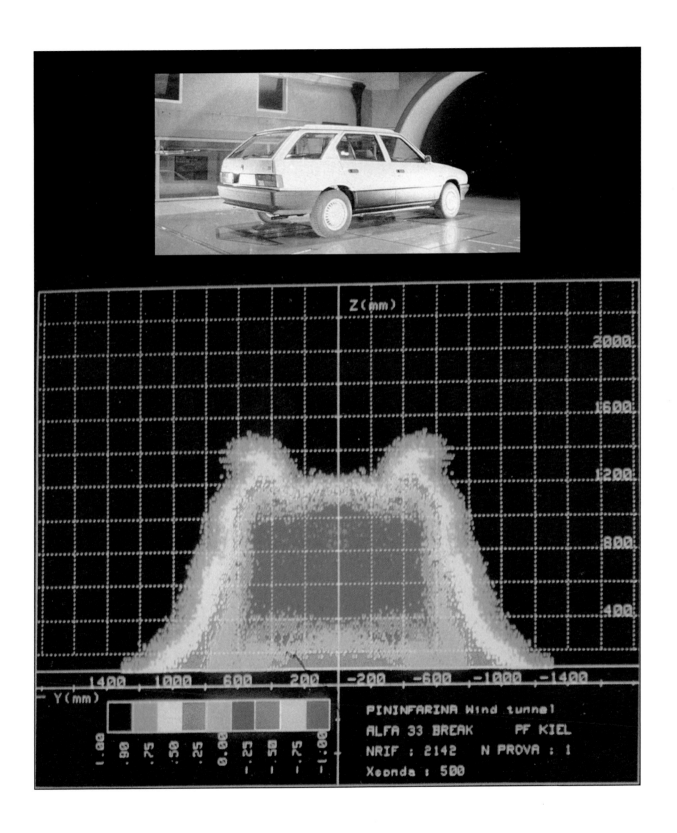

PININFARINA Wind tunnel
ALFA 33 BREAK   PF KIEL
NRIF : 2142   N PROVA : 1
Xsonda : 500

Serious Fun from BMW

There have been some surprisingly avant garde BMW models, considering the restrained character of the run-of-the-mill production Bee Emms. In the early '60s, Bertone and Michelotti both did design studies and the former was responsible for the limited edition 3200CS cars.

The BMW CSL Batmobile had a 3-litre motor and somewhat extravagant coachwork, while the BMW Turbo was a design study by Paul Bracq in 1972, which could be considered the inspiration for the M1. The latter 3½-litre car was the basis for a Group 4 racing car, and 450 were made. The M635CSi coupé uses a development of the M1 engine and is still in production, while a small run of M5 cars were made between '84 and '87 using the 635CSi power unit.

It is unlike BMW to describe *anything* as a fun car, yet that is what the company says about the seriously glamorous Z1 Roadster. This Porsche-eating two-seater was first seen in prototype form in 1986 and it is now being produced in limited numbers. Developed remarkably quickly by BMW Technik, the

For such a traditional producer, BMW's 1978 M1 sports/racer was always considered rather extravagant, but 450 were sold.

Munich firm's technical think tank, the car has a monocoque-style steel chassis and reinforced plastic floor pan and main shell. The doors slide down into the high sills electro-mechanically and there is a gas-assisted hood. The undertray controls the airflow beneath the car so effectively that the Z1 is claimed to be the first production car to achieve race-car 'ground effect' to reduce aerodynamic lift.

Another decidedly sporty Bee Emm is the M3, which is available only in l.h.d. form. Although derived from a road race car by the company's motor sport division, it is both comfortable and easy to drive, with very safe handling. Top speed is 143mph/230kmh and it is possible to catapult the M3 from zero to 60mph/100kmh in 6.7 seconds.

Perhaps it is 'only a 3 series' but it can be instantly distinguished from the lady executive's company car by its flared wheel arches, wider wheels and big spoilers. The 2.3-litre engine pushes out a smooth but insistent 200 horsepower.

Ford's Eltec

Perhaps it is debatable if the Ford Eltec ('ELectronic TEChnology') qualifies as a proto/concept type of car, but one must bear in mind the often short intervals between Ford conceptions and realizations. Certainly it is more than a dream car.

An experimental o.h.c. 12-valve 4-cyl light-alloy engine of 1.3 litres powers the front-wheel-drive 5-door functional saloon, which rather resembles an up-dated Sierra, albeit with the futuristic stamp of Ghia. Features include very large areas of flush-fitting glass, an electronically-controlled louvre-type sunroof and retractable underbody section to aid fuel economy. When the Eltec was introduced in 1985, Ford somewhat curiously claimed that the body had been designed to provide the additional interior space which would be necessary to accommodate the driver and passengers of the 21st century, 'research having shown that the average height and weight of both men and women is continuing to increase'.

The bodywork of the car is in a metallic finish claimed to provide a showroom gloss for life. An interesting feature of the

The blood line to the Sierra is clearly evident in the proto/concept Ford Eltec of 1985. Packed with electronic wizardry, it had a Ford Aerospace computer.

interior equipment is that the instrument nacelle moves with the adjustable steering column so the wheel rim cannot mask the dials. Eltec has a high-intensity headlamp system which operates rather like a slide projector, and is said to be dazzle-free. The car's Uniroyal Conti tyres are run-flat.

The Eltec has the Ford Aerospace designed EEC–IV computer, which controls the engine, the continuously variable transmission, the air suspension which reacts to both load and speed, the anti-lock braking, and engine cooling. It also continuously monitors the vehicle's entire electrical system and, by virtue of its linkage with the throttle, checks for wheelspin.

The Eltec, as Ford states, was designed to show that even modest family cars can benefit from electronic co-ordination of all their operating functions, and that the intelligent use of electronic controls can improve the dynamic characteristics of the car while reducing both fuel consumption and exhaust emissions.

Supercats

Information on Jaguar's mooted successor to the legendary E Type is still sketchy. Known in the industry as Project XJ 41 it is more popularly and rather obviously known as the F Type. Jaguar have been working on prototypes in close collaboration with FF Developments, the four-wheel-drive specialists of Coventry, England.

It seems likely that the car will be offered in 4WD form with a 400 bhp motor derived from the 6-cyl AJ6 with twin turbos, upped to 4 litres in deference to Stateside enthusiasts who find the 3.6 motor less than dramatically urgent. The F Type is said to share a basic floor deck with the XJ40 saloon but this is no reason why it should not look like an intelligent playboy's dream.

One sports car that is different in shape to the rash of similar cars for the 1990s, if the prototypes are anything to judge by, is the Panther Solo, which was conceived, then abandoned, in 1984. The subsequent offspring, the Solo 2, is

The Jaguar XJ 220 was the sensation of the 1988 Motor Show in Britain. The big concept car was part-sponsored by component manufacturers.

alive and well and living in Harlow, England. In fact it will probably be twins or triplets or a small family eventually and from all the information one can glean, it is a proposition not to be sneezed at: the firm aim to market it at a reasonable price – say £30,000/$20,000 as a thoughtful guess.

The shape of the Solo is different mainly because of the short nose, forward driving position and midships power unit. It is a very good looking car, fashioned by the British designer Ken Greenley. The beauty is far more than skin deep: the body is a composite structure of steel, honeycombed aluminium and resin reinforced by carbon fibre, glass fibre and Kevlar and there is an immensely strong although spidery frame. The nose incorporates a Formula 1-type energy absorbing system for maximum safety.

Among numerous consultants concerned with the designing of the Solo were the March Group, of Bicester, England, whose

PANTHER SIX

ABOVE an early concept from Panther Cars was the
Panther Six, with curious steering 'bogie'.

LEFT Concept/prototype for the long-awaited Panther
Solo: Ford Cosworth power and an ingenious composite
body.

racecar wizardry is legendary and who have a full-scale wind
tunnel. The car's drag factor, at Cd0.33, may not be exceptional
these days, but it is reported to have excellent downforce
because of the underbody contours and the racecar-bred wing
and spoiler.

With its 2-litre 204 bhp Ford Cosworth turbo-charged engine,
the Solo should be up among the 150mph top-speeders, and
the suspension and running gear are sophisticated enough to
ensure a brilliant handling. The transmission is via a 5-speed
manual box and transfer box to all four wheels. Braking is four-
wheel-disc with ATE anti-lock system.

Lotus

Several prototypes exist for new Lotus cars, and since the company came under the aegis of General Motors, there has been a great deal more room for manoeuvre. A new Elan is on the stocks, and the M100 'mystery car' is due for launch. Any new Lotus cars will almost certainly have active suspension. Certainly such a system exists in prototype form and not necessarily on Lotus products, since the Lotus Group serve numerous clients as consultants, initiators and developers. The Lotus version of active suspension replaces springs and shock absorbers with double-acting hydraulic units controlled by a central microprocessor, which determines their vertical movement over road irregularities.

Showing the characteristic wedge shape, the Lotus Etna prototype carries on the firm's traditions of design and construction. Lotus have used fibre-reinforced materials for over a quarter of a century. The firm are both consultants and manufacturers in automotive and other fields.

VW Beetle

The VW Beetle story is well documented. Pictures include the front and rear of the 1936/7 pre-series VW 30 which followed the historic three prototypes of October 1936. The 30 cars designated VW 30 underwent exhaustive testing right through 1937. In 1938 the Beetle appeared in its definitive form as part of test series VW 38. It was powered by a 24 bhp air-cooled Porsche boxer motor. Also illustrated, is one of the many early experimental prototypes.

Buick's Reatta:
International Cooperation

Behind one of the slickest, glamour-laced American sports cars of all time – the Buick Reatta two-place coupé – lies a fascinating story of conception and development involving five nations.

Reatta was conceived at Buick HQ in Flint, and was styled at Warren, Mich. Production is at modern plant in Lansing, Mich. The car's motor is the 3800, the latest generation of the Buick-developed 3.8-litre V-6.

Buick wanted expertise in prototype and low-volume production at a time when their own people were overloaded; a worldwide search took them to England. They had sheet-metal dies made in Japan, studied paint processes in Portugal and conducted tough prototype testing in Spain. The styling assignment reached GM Advanced Designed Studio No 2 in 1982, and a clay scale model was made and went through a series of changes before the concept glass fibre model was completed in early 1983.

ABOVE Scale model of the Reatta concept, made in 1982 by David S McIntoch of GM Design and modeller Davis Rossi.

TOP Call it, if you like, multinational. The Buick Reatta's constructors drew on American, British, Portuguese, Spanish and Japanese sources.

British firms were placed under contract in 1984. Hawtal Whiting Design and Engineering Co was signed up for engineering and prototype build. Abbey Panels, Coventry, made bodies in white and shipped them to Luton for priming. Aston-Martin Tickford painted the bodies and assembled the cars in the later stages, while the Mildenhall firm of Lamb-Sceptre were concerned with tool design and manufacture. In Japan, Ogihara Iron Works were contracted to build sheet-metal dies.

Prototype road tests, lab tests and barrier tests were done in England. Mountain and desert testing took place at various locations in Spain.

Manufacturing tooling for the body that was designed and built in England was shipped to America for installation at Lansing in a totally renovated plant which had once been part of the Oldsmobile complex.

ABOVE The charismatic Reatta has 3800 V6 motor, front wheel drive, fast-ratio power steering and anti-lock braking.

TOP RIGHT At a late development stage, this fibreglass model, minus the lift-off targa top, won GM's corporate approval.

BOTTOM RIGHT Full size clay model of the Reatta, made in January 1983. (Reatta means lariat or lassoo).

I·DE·A

When the Institute for Development in Automotive Engineering (IDEA) was formed in 1978 on the outskirts of Turin, people tended to ask if there was a need for such an establishment. The success and rapid growth of this consultancy and design 'factory' has answered the question positively, and particularly in the acclaimed success of Vettura Sperimentale a Sottosistemi (Experimental Subsystem Car).

The objectives of VSS were to design a car which would:

1 allow production using systems other than current ones, by using subsystems in such a way as to allow greater decentralization of production.

2 weigh less.

3 have a longer life.

4 allow the use of production tooling over a longer period even in case of restyling or new models.

Put simply, the idea was to abandon the idea of the monocoque or stressed outer skin concept, and substitute an inner tub or cage of steel, with outer member in lightweight materials, probably plastic.

This separation of functions allows many possibilities in terms of shape, materials and assembly methods.

For the same external dimensions, the body of the VSS prototype weighs at least 20% less than a conventional car built with all-steel components. Leading chemical industries have taken part in the project by studying and preparing plastics featuring high mechanical properties as well as maximum lightness, in both thermoplastic and thermosetting materials.

TOP LEFT Villa Cantamerla, handsome HQ of the I.DE.A Institute in Moncalieri, outside Turin.

TOP RIGHT Silvano Botta, supervisor of the Models and Prototypes workshop.

TOP RIGHT The pace car serves as a mobile test vehicle for
Ferrari, and is an important exercise in the development
of a 2+2 mid-engined road car.

TOP LEFT Base structure for the experimental subsystem
car, the VSS, by I.DE.A.

ABOVE The VSS working prototype used the existing mechanical
units of Fiat's Ritmo but with a 20% weight reduction.

LEFT Ferrari pace car for the PPG/Indy Cart
Race Series was set up by I.DE.A.

PININFARINA

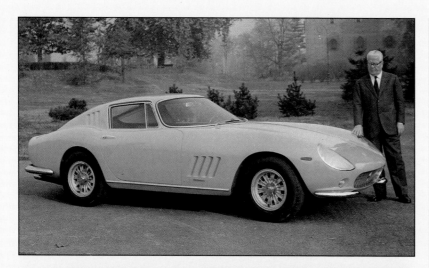

The immortal Battista Pininfarina with one of his creations – the Ferrari 275 GTB.

ABOVE A real trendsetter by Pininfarina was the Cisitalia 2-seat coupe of 1947, when European manufacturers were just re-awakening.

Acknowledged as the most prestigious of the Italian coachbuilders and styling houses, the name of Pininfarina is synonymous with style. Battista Farina himself was born in 1893, as the first cars took to the road and died in 1966. He acquired the nickname Pinin ('Little One'). Professionally, he and his firm used the name Farina initially (hence, for example, the Farina-bodied Austin and Morris cars of the early 1960s). In 1961, however, Farina officially changed his name to Pininfarina. The Pininfarina of today is his son Sergio, President and Managing Director of Pininfarina Industrie SpA, Cassella Postale 295, 10100 Turin.

Early in his career, Battista befriended the automotive pioneers Lancia and Ferrari, who were enthusiastic racers and subsequently manufacturers. After he had visited the States in 1922, he set up as a coachbuilder, with the support of Lancia and Ferrari. By 1939 Carrozzeria Farina had 500 employees and was making bodies for 800 cars a year.

Distinctive Pininfarina shapes were beginning to be seen, in the slightly angular but attractive and aerodynamic lines of cars such as the Lancia Aprilia and Aurelia, and some of the Cisitalia models. The firm was not only manufacturing bodies and

converting existing designs but
was also acting as consultant to
major manufacturers, a state of
affairs which holds today.

Because of his friendship with
Ferrari and Lancia and because
they were all members of the
Torinese elite of automobile
creators, Pininfarina continued
to have close consultancy
contracts with these men and
their companies and he and the
firm became almost identifiable
with the charismatic Ferrari
'prancing horse' stable, being
responsible for the design of the
Testarossa, 250, 275 and 330
GT, Dino, Daytona, Mondial and
other models. Today, the firm
still have close links with Ferrari,
whilst their skill and flair are
sought in many other areas.

TOP One of the most eyeable of all the Ferraris –
the 1984 308 GTO.

ABOVE Prototype Y, a four-door three-wheeler with
'1960s' (actually 1961) written all over it.

RIGHT Classic prancing horse badge of the marque Ferrari
includes the Italian tricolor.

GIUGIARO

TOP Good-looking Lotus Etna was a concept/prototype with styling by Giugiaro and consultants Ital Design.

ABOVE Giugiaro (in the light suit) and Chapman with Lotus.

To the average auto enthusiast, the name of Giugiaro is probably best known today in connection with the increasingly popular SEAT range of cars which were blessed with his consultancy at the design stage. In the early 1970s, however, the designer's genius could be clearly identified in the Alfa Romeo Alfasud and the Volkswagen Passat and Golf. Since then his work and that of Ital Design, the company which he set up in 1968, has extended a great deal further, embracing such marques as Audi, Fiat, Lancia and BMW.

Giorgetto Giugiaro's career started in 1950, when he studied at the Academia di Belle Arti in Turin, working in Fiat's design department to pay his fees.

In 1960 he joined the Bertone consultancy/construction firm, working on such marques as Aston Martin, Ferrari, Mazda and Dino. Subsequently progressing to head of styling at the illustrious Ghia, he designed such exotica as the Maserati Merak and Ghibli. By 1972 he was concerned with the creation of the Alfa Romeo Alfetta and Alfasud and was regarded as the most promising of the younger generation of designers in the automotive field.

Shortly after he set up his own firm, with Aldo Mantovani and Luciano Bosio, he earned fame (or notoriety) for the semi-concept Manta Bizzarini shown at the Turin salon. A few years later he was working on more realistic projects including the Lotus Esprit.

TOP The much-celebrated Lotus Esprit Turbo came into being in 1981, styled by Giugiaro.

RIGHT The utterly functional yet beautiful cockpit of the Lotus Esprit.

BOTTOM The futuristic Boomerang concept car.

BERTONE

ABOVE RIGHT Typical Bertone styling for
the Mazda 323 Turbo.

ABOVE Bertone badging on the
Lamborghini Miura.

One of the greatest successes
of Nuccio Bertone was the
shaping of the small Fiat X1/9
roadster which, although now
obsolescent, has become
something of a classic. It first
appeared at Turin in 1969 in the
form of a prototype/concept fun
car, but went into production in
1972 as a less dramatic and
unquestionably serious mid-
motor two-seater with targa top.

Mention Bertone to most
people and that is the car they
will think of. They may not know,
or may have forgotten, that he
designed the Lamborghini
Countach of 1973 – one of the
most exotic supercars of all time
and still going strong. It was
around this time that he was
reported as saying: 'The wind in
our factory blows now hot now
cold . . . . personally I am not
directly influenced by this state
of affairs because I have thrown

up a barrier between Bertone
the designer and Bertone the
industrialist . . . . I can even
manage to unload my nervous
tension when I am designing.
For me it has become almost a
hobby.'

Whatever he may have felt,
Bertone has always had a sense
of responsibility as well as
delight, and has been much
concerned with automotive
safety in his creations.

He was involved with the
recent exceptionally safety-
conscious Volvo 480 semi-sports
car, and the 1975 264TE. Then
there was the 262 coupe of
1977, Bertone-designed and
celebrating Volvo's 50th
birthday.

Today, Carrozzeria Bertone
SpA, Corse Allamano 46, Turin,
can take credit for the styling of
the first really new Skoda car for
years – the Favorit.

LEFT The Bertone-designed Fiat X1/9 – a highly successful roadster.

BELOW A classic supercar still in production – the Lamborghini Countach.

BOTTOM LEFT Aggressive yet aesthetic – the 1968 Lamborghini Miura.

chapter three

DREAMS CARS AND EXOTICA

A beautifully styled concept car from Peugeot – the Oxia.
The mid-mounted engine allows remarkable forward
vision.

Among exotica, Porsche 959 surely merits description more than most. Here is a car which you are unlikely to find for sale, yet it is a very real product, and with persistance and a lot of money (try 425,000 Dm) a person could possess one, because it is a listed low-production model.

Originally a 1983 Porsche 911 Group B sports car design study, it became a 1984 rally winner from which the 959 prototype was developed and entered in the 1985 Dakar Rally, showing great promise but being defeated after smashing into several large boulders. Porsche were so confident as to conduct road tests for a series of 200 for delivery to buyers during 1986. Since then there have been only minor modifications. Production is still small, and the beautiful beast comes only left-hand-drive, but it could reasonably be considered the flagship of the range.

The car is technically very interesting. It is based on a rear-engine format with all-wheel drive, a concept dictated by its

ABOVE Probably the most exciting of the Porsche models, the 959 – intended as a user-friendly road car as well as a sports racer.

RIGHT Porsche's 959 specialized Group C two-seater race car, with mid-mounted Flat-six engine and twin turbochargers, and tenuous links to the original 911 Turbo road car.

use as a rally machine as well as road car. According to the Porsche Research and Development Centre at Weissach, however, the electronically-controlled system for optimum dynamics perfects 4WD for everyday motoring. This electronic control ensures variable power transmission to the front or rear axles, depending on road surface conditions. Although the drive programme can be called up by the driver, it can also be overridden to meet any need.

Cutaway of the Porsche 959 at the Earl's Court Motor Show, 1986.

The engine is a 935 and 936 world championship car derivative, and is a twin turbo-charged 2.85-litre boxer six with water-cooled heads and air-cooled block, four valves per cylinder and double o.h. cams per bank. Power output is 400 bhp and this is transmitted to the transaxle system through a six-speed gearbox.

The chassis of the Group B car features the latest Porsche racecar technology with dual wishbone suspension and adjustable stabilisers all round. Also, as on the 1984 World Championship-winning Porsche 956, there are Dunlop Denloc safety runflat tyres with unusually-sized 17in. wheel rims. The modified Porsche 911 Turbo bodywork was perfected in the wind tunnel and offers a Cd value of 0.32 for minimal air restistance and good downforce.

Performance figures quoted for the car are a zero to 62.5mph time of 3.9 secs, a zero to 125mph time of 14.8 seconds and a top speed of 196mph, so the 959 must be one of the fastest of all road cars, tantalisingly close to the claim of 'fastest ever'.

It is interesting to note that two-stage supercharging is employed. That is to say, instead of the more usual arrangement of two parallel blowers for high performance cars, Porsche use two turbos in series. One of them operates the entire rev range. When more exhaust energy is available at higher revs, the other blower, which has already been accelerated, provides additional boost.

Although this is an out-and-out competitve sports car, Porsche have stated that any driver of average experience, male or female, can handle a 959 easily and without a long learning phase, but buyers are offered driver courses and additional training if required.

In future developments, state the firm, they will not be promising the fully automatic car, but rather the support systems which a driver can call on when a need arises. Such systems offer drivers learning potential and decision options. Although many advances in vehicle technology have been introduced in

Boldly, NSU of Germany adopted the remarkable Wankel rotary engine in their Ro80 of 1967. The twin-rotor mill gave 130bhp.

the 959, operation of the controls remains simple, the cockpit hardly differing from that of a 911. Excessive presentation of secondary information was intentionally avoided. The driver's direct range of vision includes easily-read analogue dials plus nothing more than a functions display for drivetrain control. The switch for selecting the drivetrain programme, used to optimize the all-wheel drive surface adhesion, is handily placed between the steering wheel and gear lever. Less often needed switches for adjustment of shock absorbers or vehicle height are located on the central console, still well within the driver's reach.

A significant and unusual feature in the 959 is the air pressure control system to monitor tyres and wheels, developed by Porsche and Bosch with support from the German Federal Ministry for Research and Technology. It has been used in Porsche racecars since 1980.

Damaged tyres or cracks in wheels are registered as an air pressure loss. The spokes of the magnesium wheels are hollow, forming a common air chamber with the tyres. Switches are built into each wheel, reacting to air pressure in the tyre.

Faded Dreams

Some dream cars are also lost causes. Such was the ill-starred Chrysler turbine of 1964. Let us be clear about the word turbine in this context. It has nothing to do with the exhaust-driven turbines so popular today. The Chrysler had a gas turbine engine similar in principle to those used on propeller turbine aircraft of that era. Ford and Rover had experimental gas turbines but although there were some effective commercial vehicle turbines, the idea never caught on for cars, partly because of high fuel consumption.

The car was designed by Chrysler in America and hand-built by Ghia of Turin, with a turbine motif. Thus the headlamps were set in chrome rings which simulated turbine wheels and

The Mazda RX-7: keeping faith with the Wankel rotary engine. The Turbo (above) worked in two stages to combat turbo lag, opening a second chamber so that the gases could drive all of the turbine blades, rather than just a section, above 2,500 rmp. ABS (anti-lock brake system) was an option on the Turbo model. Electromagnetic sensors (above right) at each wheel relayed braking action to a microprocessor which modulated braking to avoid wheel lock-up and improve stability.

the symbolism was repeated at the rear end in ribbed tubes housing the reversing lamps. The wheels had a decorative turbine wheel design on white sidewalls. Having tested the car, I have to admit that Chrysler's turbine supplied power with an uncanny lack of vibration, very much in the manner of the Wankel rotary which, perhaps less probably, had a future.

Nobody really believed NSU when they said, in the early 1960s, that they had built the most revolutionary car in the world – the NSU Spider powered by a Wankel rotary engine. They added: 'This is no prototype shown to cause a stir and then be forgotten', and they could have been right because a subsequent development of the car was the twin-Wankel Ro80 saloon which was in production until 1977 with a total of 37,000 cars manufactured.

The Ro80 was a very advanced car with electronic ignition, semi-automatic transmission, disc brakes front and rear, and power steering. It really was a nice car, and it was a pity NSU never overcame the sealing and fuel consumption problems, but Mazda took up the cause of the rotary engine with conspicuous success, culminating in today's RX7 fast roadster.

Concept Car or Restyle?
Lotus Carlton

One of the more exciting new models announced in 1988 was the Lotus Carlton, developed by Lotus Engineering of Norwich, England, and Vauxhall/Opel, badged outside the UK as the Lotus Omega.

An important partner in the worldwide operations of General Motors, Lotus also helped to develop the 387 bhp V8 motor for the new Chevy Corvette ZR1, whilst Vauxhall and Team Lotus jointly established the Vauxhall Lotus challenge series, started in 1988. Like the Corvette, the Lotus Carlton/Omega typifies the high-performance cars now in increasing demand in Europe and the US.

The car is powered by a 3.6-litre 6-cyl engine with 24 valves and twin turbochargers, developing 360 bhp at 5800 rpm. Production will be on the basis of a limited series. A car of this

ABOVE The multiple-valve powerhouse of the MR2.

ABOVE Exploded version of the Alfa ProCar shows the muscular mid-mounted engine.

TOP It looks mild and innocent enough, but the Alfa Romeo ProCar can hit 215 mph.

type can be considered more in the nature of exotica, since it is the inspired modification of an existing design rather than concept or prototype.

While not of notably futuristic design, but rather more a macho-looking saloon, the car embodies several advanced features including a new ignition system that does not need a distributor, but has three ignition coils rather than one, each serving two spark plugs. The Lotus Carlton also has two closed-loop catalytic converters of metal monolith type to keep exhaust emissions to a minimum.

In order to make the fullest possible use of the torque and power reserves, a six-speed gearbox similar to that of the Corvette ZR1 is being used. Because of the beefy torque, (376 lbs/ft) a new type of clutch embodies a diaphragm spring which is not compressed, as is normally the case, but is pulled. This reduces pedal effort, as well as increasing contact pressure. Larger front and rear spoilers distinguish the car from the luxury saloon on which it is based, and there are important-looking flared wheel arches. The spoilers increase the aero-dynamic downthrust. At speeds of over 100mph/160kmh the

rear spoiler automatically extends to reduce lift. Drag coefficient is Cd 0.30.

Which one is the real 164? A production version of the 164 – the 3-litre V6 De Lusso.

Prototypes that Aren't

There is a class of car, quite officially and unequivocally called a prototype, which is frequently nothing of the kind. I refer to specially built, terribly expensive sports cars the purpose of which is not only to win races, but to serve as mobile test beds. Le Mans winners have for many years come into this category, and the World Sportscar Championship has demanded specialist machines of this type. The matter has been put concisely in the *Pirelli Album of Motor Sport*, in the following terms:

'At Le Mans, most of the pretence had been discarded; it was a race for 'prototypes' – cars which just conceivably could be distantly related to something which might possibly be put into production one day . . .'

Such cars, accordingly, are more or less dreamlike, and ordinary mortals are very unlikely ever to get their hands on such priceless objects. Consider the Nimrod Aston, which looked perhaps more like a cruise missile than a motorcar. It was created by Nimrod Racing, with the simple aim of winning at Le Mans, where the last Aston-Martin engined car won in 1959. The aim was not achieved, but the car was used for other long-distance events with some distinction.

An interesting inversion of the process of building a 'funny' car which might one day become the basis of something more conventional, is seen in Alfa Romeo's dramatically understated 215mph/346kmh ProCar – a competition machine designed to look exactly like an Alfa 164 saloon. The result of a joint venture by Brabham and Alfa Romeo, the 164 ProCar has been built as a feasibility study for a new formula of motor sport. To comply with the FISA'S proposed regulations for such a formula, the car must exactly resemble a current high-volume production automobile, but the chassis and mechanicals can be completely different.

LEFT A rarity from the Pininfarina styling studios, with a distinctive front end: the 1975 Alfa Romeo Eagle Spider.

ABOVE 0-60mph in 3.8 seconds: the legendary Shelby Cobra.

Outwardly, the car is a carbon fibre plastic replica of the 164, even to badges, wipers, indicators, door locks etc. Under the skin it uses the latest competition technology, with a 3.5-litre V10 mid-mounted engine driving the rear wheels. As on a Formula 1 car, the ProCar has a central cockpit of composite construction. Horsepower is over 600, compared with the 192 bhp of the 164. 0-60mph takes just over two seconds . . .

The Best in The World

One of the all-time greats among simple, almost brutal open sports cars was the Shelby Cobra, which, in 1963, was developed from the British AC Ace designed by Tojeiro. In the Carroll Shelby form it had a 4.7-litre Ford V8 motor which you would think would give enough muscle, but Shelby American Inc

The Cobra was never put into mass production: each car was carefully built up by hand and each one was, in consequence, different to any other. The 90 degree V8 engine – particularly in its bigblock 427ci guise – gave so much power to the Cobra that drag racing rules were changed in the US to keep it out.

upped it to 7 litres so that enthusiasts could really summon up the adrenalin and alarm themselves and others. One motoring journalist reported back: 'I bought the 427 from Shelby on the spot and gave a check, using my driver's license for identification. We both realized that it might be the last time either of us would see the document.'

In the 1970s, the Cobra became a cult machine. Shelby were no longer making them, but used cars were restored or became the subjects of replicas, usually in glass fibre, although the original was aluminium-panelled. A British engineer, Brian Angliss, improved on this decadent practice by acquiring the original Cobra patterns and wooden bucks and produced virtual replicas, albeit with milder engines. The cars were craftsman-built in a small factory at the historic Brooklands race track, itself the subject of renaissance as a museum and heritage site.

The TVR cult started as far back as 1957 but it was the
Ford V8-motored Griffith of 1962 that really got the
marque off the ground.

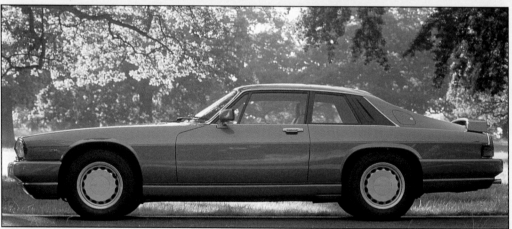

The XJR-S was more or less an exuberant shout of victory by Jaguar Sport after Jaguar's win at Le Mans in 1988. A dream car? In terms of performance and rarity, it fits the bill, if a saloon can ever be a dream car.

Two years ago, Ford reached an agreement witn Angliss for the construction of a new development and manufacturing centre for his firms, Autokraft and AC Cars, and announced that AC were developing a 140mph/225kmh 4-wheel-drive 2-seater sports car to be known as the AC Ace and a prototype was shown at the UK Motor Show in October 1986. In the meantime Autokraft would continue to make Cobras, although they couldn't legally use that name, as it was Shelby's property.

Powered by a Ford V6 2.9-litre fuel-injected Granada motor, the Ace also uses the Granada's all-wheel-drive running gear and incorporates a wide range of other Ford components such as suspension, instrumentation, lighting, heating and air-conditioning.

The chassis was designed by former Ford high-performance engineer Len Bailey, who had worked on the classic Le Mans winning Ford GT cars. The aerodynamic body and detachable hardtop were created by Ford's European design staff.

'Handcrafted British sports cars since 1949' is the proud boast of TVR Engineering Ltd., Blackpool, England. TVR's story actually began in 1947 when the 23-year-old auto enthusiast Trevor Wilkinson rebuilt an Alvis Firebird with an alloy 2-seat body of racy, seductive contours. He called it TVR, culling the letters from his own given name.

By 1949 he was making his own tubular chassis and panelled sports bodies, using Ford or Coventry Climax engines, and selling kits as well as complete cars. By 1955 there was growing interest Stateside and a TVR coupé was featured at the 1957 New York Auto Show. A year later the Grantura was launched, representing the culmination of two years testing and racing in North America, and TVR went into serious if limited series production.

In the 1960s the TVR Tuscan and Griffith, with husky V8 motors, were challenging such exotica as Jaguar and Ferrari sports racers. Export success in the USA continued with the 2500M, mounting a Triumph 2.5-litre engine and in the UK the Vixen and Tuscan V6 were powered by Ford engines and followed by the 3000M. The end of the '70s saw the introduction of a turbo V6 of 230 bhp, claimed as the first British car to have exhaust supercharging on a regular production basis.

In 1980 the all-new Tasmin rag top and convertible delighted the faithful band of TVR fans and in 1984 the 390 Special Equipment models pumped out 275 bhp from 3.9 litres of V8.

TVR now list half a dozen pulse-quickening models, including the S Convertible, first shown as a styling concept in 1986, and the TVR 420 SEAC – standing for Special Equipment Aramid Composite. The latter has been developed from the TVR team

Secrecy is often a part of the development of new models, usually not through any fear of industrial espionage, but rather to help the marketing men make the maximum impact on release. The new Jaguar XJ40s were tested wearing crude camouflage panels.

racecars, with extended bore and stroke producing 4228 cc capacity and 300 bhp. Lightweight body materials including Kevlar reduce overall mass, resulting in better performance and aerodynamic styling with a large rear wing to increase downforce, thus aiding roadholding and handling. A ready-to-race TVR is the Tuscan Challenge Convertible of which only 30 have been made for the one-make challenge event. No less a dream car, but somewhat less specialized, is the 2801 Convertible Series 3 Automatic – the only TVR that is available with automatic transmission and complies with all current US safety and emission regulations. The latest Series 3 features an integrated front air dam with new light units and impact absorbing bumpers. Revised side sills are moulded into the body shell and there is a new bonnet.

To put TVR in perspective, one cannot perhaps do better than quote the firm's own comment on its production, in the following terms:

'In an age when cars are turned out by robots in a matter of hours, TVR is the glorious exception. Instead of racing off the production line, it's made at a snail's pace almosty entirely by hand. Indeed the whole pains-taking process takes over four hundred hours, a consider-able portion of which is spent honing the body to its final glass-like finish. Of course you can't build cars like this by the millions so every year we only create a few hundred. A degree of rarity we feel will reflect the type of owner.'

To dream is one thing. To be able to buy a dream car is another. How to buy a Jaguar XJR-9? Forget it. No way. The beautiful racecars will stay with their masters. Consolation might be found in an XJR-S, created by the Oxford firm of Jaguar Sport.

One of Jaguar Sport's first customers was Jan Lammers, who won the 1988 Le Mans race with the XJR-9. The XJR-S was announced to celebrate the victory and Lammers at once ordered one. In fact he took delivery of car number 002, the same number as the Le Mans winner.

The XJR-S is a fully engineered sports coupé developed from the XJ-S. With its V12 5.3-litre 286 bhp motor, it will squirt from zero to 60mph in 7½ seconds and will cruise at over 150mph if you can find somewhere to do such a thing.

Power is taken through a 3-speed automatic transmission and a limited slip differential. Cruise control gives totally relaxed motoring. Anti-lock braking is standard. Suspension is scientifically beefed-up and there are special wheels and tyres. The aerodynamics are improved by the air dam and spoiler, rear apron and deep door-sill mouldings.

There is another Jaguar – the Lister – the creators of which are not afraid to claim it as 'Probably the Best Jaguar in the World'. To some of the best-heeled dreamers in the globe, it may be just that.

Lister, a specialist converter of Leatherhead, Surrey, offers several variants, but the flagship (or dreamship?) is based on the XJS and is described as a car built from experience and knowledge of the desires of the true driving enthusiast for a car which provides all the luxury and refinement of a touring car together with the power and handling of a race car. Lister go on to sing its praises in the following terms: 'A car in which it is possible to hear the stereo above the roar of the V12 engine – a car which will happily idle in traffic jams or fly past the rest on the open road – a car in which to travel long distances in comfort – an individual car.'

Engine of the Lister is the Jaguar V12 up-rated by lengthening the stroke from 70 to 78.5mm, thus increasing the capacity from 5343 cc to 5995 cc and giving a power output of 482 bhp at 6000 rpm instead of 300 bhp at 5,000. Lister claim an acceleration figure of 5.4 secs for zero to 60mph and a top speed of 170mph. All Lister engines are hand-built and dynamo-meter-tested. The latest manifestation is the Le Mans, and this is even more powerful by virtue of a 7-litre 12-cyl motor pushing out over 500 bhp and 540 lb ft of torque. Although a hand-crafted supercar in the mould of the Ferrari F40, it can seat four people. The all-steel body is a carefully conceived

Perhaps the most glamorous and practical convertible available today – the Mercedes-Benz 300 SL.

LEFT The Chevrolet Corvette in two forms – pre-ZR-1 and ZR-1 (foreground). The engine of the ZR-1 is a 5.7-litre Lotus-developed unit.

ABOVE The rear end is more rounded than on previous Corvettes. Fat, low-profile tyres transfer the extra power to the road.

styling tour de force intended both to reduce drag and improve safety while providing space and comfort. It was tested and proved by CAD (Computer Aided Design). Each car will be guaranteed capable of a 200mph top speed.

Suspension and braking are, of course, suitably modified for these cars and have been proven by W P Automotive, manufacturers of the Lister range, with their own XJS race car which has competed successfully at many events worldwide.

If I were making a shopping list of contemporary dream cars, I would have to include the Corvette ZR1, the Mercedes 300 or 500 SL, a Ferrari F40, a Lamborghini and a De Tomaso. The new Corvette is so powerful that it has two different start keys – one of which you hide if junior or even first lady wants to drive . . . The V8 5.7-litre motor is Lotus-developed, and made by Mercury Marne, Oklahoma. The whole car is beefier and more aggressive than a normal Corvette.

The Ferrari F40, possibly the fastest, most expensive and most exciting car in the world today, can rocket from zilch to 124mph in 12 seconds and terminal speed is just above 200mph. The beauteous body is in carbon fibre and Kevlar composite over a tube space-frame.

The Lamborghini is still one of the world's supercars, although

ABOVE Probably the fastest and most expensive
production sports car of recent years has been the
Ferrari F40. The engine develops 480 bhp. The body
is plastic.

LEFT The carbon-fibre and glass-mat body is glued to a
multi-tubular space frame, giving optimum torsional
stiffness.

a new model is needed and expected. The Countach has been the most successful model. It was introduced in 1973 and is due to be replaced by the Diablo quite soon.

The De Tomaso? Yes, both the car and the man are still around. I know because I saw them on a recent visit to Modena, the Northern Italian motoring shrine. With De Tomaso when I met him was the great Froilan Gonzales – the 'Pampas Bull' of grand prix racing. The De Tomaso Pantera may be showing its age now, but it is still a classic Italian supercar. It has a mid-mounted 5¾-litre motor and the handling is exceptional.

The Mercedes-Benz new 300/500 SL range is in the nature of a born-again version of one of the prettiest and most celeb-rated Mercedes ever – the 300 SL Gull Wing of 1954. The new car bristled with advanced features, including an automatic roll-over bar which pops up at the hint of an accident. The lovely car comes with the option of an electrically-operated soft top or an electro-magnetically attached light-alloy hard top. Beauty, of course, is in the eye of the beholder; such lists are really a game anyone can play.

ABOVE The fabulous-looking (and performing) Countach has for years been Lamborghini's most successful seller.

ABOVE RIGHT Exotic, high-performance De Tomaso cars are still in limited production.

BELOW RIGHT A 1980 De Tomaso Pantera, stylist Guarino Bertocchi at the wheel. Very high prices are paid for these cars. Could such a dream machine, with its 5¾-litre mid-mounted engine, be anything but Italian?

Mitsubishi

The remarkable Mitsubishi HSR (High Speed Research)
car has a body inspired by the contours of the tiny
tropical humming bird.

Mitsubishi Motors design engineers used the tiny, exotic form of the tropic hummingbird as their inspiration for the 200mph HSR (High Speed Research) vehicle, which boasts a drag co-efficient of only Cd0.20. The car caused a sensation at the 1987 Tokyo Motor Show and many of its features were rapidly translated into the Mitsubishi Galant Sedan range – Japan's Car of the Year 1988 – and the 1989 Galant 4WD/4WS, described as the only production car in the world to feature 4WD and 4WS, plus advanced anti-lock braking and self-aligning suspension.

Because of the low aerodynamic drag and excellent traction, an abnormally high performance motor was not considered necessary, but the 2-litre DOHC unit gives a very useful 295 psi at the unusually high 8000 rpm.

The basic structure of the HSR is a monocoque with steel panels. The upper cabin structure is made up of a light tubular frame of high rigidity. In addition, subframes of steel tube are attached at front and rear, making it a hybrid structure. For the outer skin, lightweight high-rigidity Kevlar and polycarbonate are used.

The firm make much of what they call the Dynamic Integrated Performance System, comprising a high-technology group of 4WD, 4WS, 4IS (independent suspension), 4ABS (anti-lock braking) and Dynamic ECS (electronic control suspension). This, say Mitsubishi, is not simply the addition of individual technical features, but their integration so as to extract optimum performance.

The ability of the driver is enhanced by providing an intelligent support system, the key to which is OCS (Overall Operating Control System) whereby a high-performance multi-functional host computer is used. It thus becomes possible, say Mitsubishi, for an ordinary driver with average skills to drive safely and comfortably at speeds of around 200mph/320kmh, which is beyond the speed of normal human response. The computer controls mechanical functions and also service functions such as navigation, communications, plus monitoring systems.

ABOVE Yes, this is a steering 'wheel' on the HSR car. Some day, all cars will be built this way; or maybe not.

TOP Swoopy design concept by Aldo Sessaro, based on the Mitsubishi Colt.

Toyota FXV-11

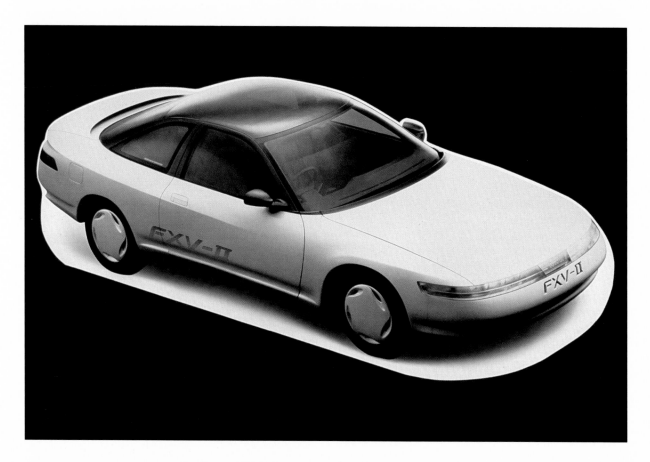

The Toyota FXV-11 is representative of Japanese automotive thinking and project progression, and is as 'slippery' and good-looking as any concept car. Features include an all-glass liquid-crystal-impregnated roof giving the driver control over admitted sunlight, automatic wipers, thin-film defoggers and defrosters, 12-way power driving seat, and Toyota multi-information system. The 4-camshaft DOHC 32-valve experimental V8 motor is based on the well-proven 4-valve motors, with silicon-aluminium alloy block and forced oil-cooled pistons.

Toyota FXV-11 glass bubble roof is crystal-impregnated, allowing control of the light entering the car by the driver.

One Man's White Elephant

If the Bugatti Royale – officially designated the Model 41 – was in any way a concept car, the concept was a very simple one. Ettore Bugatti, in the middle 1920s, had the obsession that he must build a bigger, better and more expensive car than a Rolls-Royce or a Hispano Suiza.

But the Royale wasn't a concept car, because it was intended from the start that it should go into production. It was a dream car – a piece of exotica – a legend-to-be. Bugatti seriously intended to make at least 25 of the elephantine machines, but in fact only six were ever made, between 1927 and 1933, and one of them was a prototype, in the sense that it was mechanically slightly different from those that followed.

All the cars met Bugatti's aim of upstaging Rolls Royce and Hispano Suiza, in cost and dimensions if not quality, although they were of course individually built to a very high standard. They were magnificent motorcars and Bugatti cashed in on the idea that they might be thought elephantine by using a rampant tusker as a mascot, showing rather less delicacy than Rolls Royce with their 'spirit of ecstacy' silver lady.

Model 41, the Bugatti Royale; the 15-litre engine of the prototype was scaled down to a mere 12.7 litres in production, no doubt in an attempt to cut fuel costs.

There was an ambitious and ultimately unfulfilled wish behind the choice of name. Bugatti was convinced that he could sell such a magnificent and costly machine to monarchs and maharajas. He was disappointed, because there were no takers among the royals, although King Alfonso of Spain and King Carol of Rumania were credited with 'expressing interest'.

The Royale was just over 24ft/7.3m long and had a wheelbase of 14ft/4.3m. The engine of the prototype was a 15-litre affair, but the production cars (or, if you like, the succeeding prototypes, since they were all hand-built) had a 12.7-litre unit with three valves for each of its eight cylinders, and a single overhead camshaft. That airship-derived engine weighed as much as an Austin Seven but the 7ft/2m bonnet of the car gave plenty of room for 6ft of motor. Power output was about 275 bhp at a lazy 2000 rpm and the car's top speed was about 125mph/200kmh. Price was £6500 at a time when a decent house cost £500. Today you are talking about six to nine million pounds ($9.2–12.7 million) if you can find a Royale . . .

chapter four

THE WAY AHEAD

Supercar by Honda. Codenamed NS-X it is a mid-motored
300 bhp coupe with traction control.

ABOVE Ford Europe's follow-up of prototypes has always been fast. This Probe III is not far short of the Sierra XR4.

RIGHT Ford RS 200, prototype-classification competition car.

Concept cars and prototypes almost always embody features, components and systems so advanced as to be considered futuristic or even bizarre. In many cases these abort, or lie dormant for years, but sometimes they are adopted on production cars so quickly as to take everyone by surprise.

This tends particularly to be the case if a car manufacturer engages in motor sport. There is nothing quite like racing and rallying or record-breaking to improve the breed – to accelerate technological progress – provided a well-mounted and well-funded campaign is undertaken.

Four wheel drive for roadgoing cars is admittedly hardly new. The first 4WD car appeared 80 years ago and it is almost a quarter of a century since Jensen introduced the exciting but less than successful FF luxury car with drive to all wheels. The real breakthrough took place only a few years ago, however, when championship rally winners such as Audi and Lancia derived production road-going 4WD from their highly expensive and sophisticated (virtually prototye) rally cars.

Today, permanent or selectable 4WD is offered by an increasing number of manufacturers of family and luxury cars and is regarded as an important safety factor, especially if combined with some sophisticated traction control system.

ABOVE Machimoto is the given name for this Haldesign
fun car which also tests control systems.

LEFT A very mobile test bed for systems and
components – the Lancia Delta rally car.

Mercedes-Benz, for example, on some of their models have an 'intelligent' 4WD system which decides for the driver when he needs the extra traction of 4WD – when cornering very fast or driving on slippery roads or ice, or making a fast take-off. The same cars feature anti-lock brakes and automatic locking differential, the latter a further aid to traction in wheelspin conditions. A combination of the latest mechanical and hydraulic systems is teamed with 'thinking electronics' in these cars.

Saab have developed a traction control system – TCS – which is claimed to offer advantages over other anti-wheelspin systems. By interactive control of the brakes and throttle, through the use of a microprocessor rather than the traditional mechanical throttle linkage, engine power is limited to a level that can be handled by each driving wheel. It has been developed by Saab in collaboration with brake specialists Teves and electronic experts Hella.

4WD, 4WS and Anti-lock Braking

There is certainly a whole book to be written on the subject of four-wheel drive, especially now that it has become almost commonplace. Between the world wars, Mercedes-Benz, Bugatti and Miller were among 4WD pathfinders, but it was the versatile Irish engineer Harry Ferguson who really put it on the map in the 1930s when he and Freddie Dixon constructed a race car prototype with all-wheel drive. Dixon and Tony Rolt, another racer, later built a 4WD prototype called the Crab, a remarkable feature of which was also a form of four-wheel steering.

Ferguson's team of research and development men built a single-seat formula race car, the P99, in 1961. It was driven by Stirling Moss, the first man to win a race in a 4WD car. But the road to production 4WD cars started with the prototype for a Jensen coupé in 1964 and in the remarkably short space of time of twelve months, the first Jensen FF rolled off the modest production line at West Bromwich England.

The Jensen FF was a very handsome car, with Vignale styling and a 6.3-litre 'muscle' engine. Another feature that made it remarkable and highlighted the relationship between

113

ABOVE Testing anti-lock braking system on a Ford Granada. ABS is now big business for specialized component manufacturers.

concept and production was the use of Dunlop Maxaret anti-lock braking, almost 20 years ahead of its common adoption.

Modern anti-lock braking systems are much more reliable and sophisticated and have been designed and developed largely by specialised component manufacturers such as Dunlop, Clayton Dewandre, Bendix, Automotive Products, Lucas and Alfred Teves. The component manufacturers also liaise closely with designers and manufacturers on transmission systems including four-wheel drive and four-wheel steering.

The curious thing is that four-wheel steering was almost unthinkable a decade ago. If people thought about it at all, they thought about cars that would slot into parking spots as though they were mechanical crabs, and they usually dismissed the idea as moonshine. Well – all-wheel steering is very much here today, but the crabs so far show a marked reluctance to execute swift cross-chassés on the parking lot.

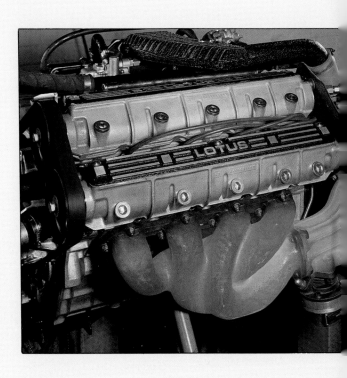

ABOVE One technological innovation that certainly stood the test of time: testing a Lotus turbocharged engine almost to the point of meltdown.

TOP, FAR RIGHT Ford proudly displays its 4×4 Granada at the London motor show, 1986. At that time, 4WD was certainly something to shout about.

RIGHT AND BELOW RIGHT If you've got it, flaunt it: Mazda 626 4WS.

Ford Granada 4x4, 1988.

Lamborghini LM is a revised Cheetah with American
Motors V8 power unit and all-wheel drive.

The point about today's all-wheel steering is not that its primary aim is to ease parking, although it does that to a useful extent, but that it improves handling right up to the car's top speed. Indeed it can be a most valuable safety feature – for example in strong side winds, on slippery surfaces and when lane-changing or taking avoiding action at motorway speeds.

With the Honda system on the Prelude the wheels are steered either in the same or the opposite direction, depending upon the amount of lock applied. In practice, this means that at anything more than low speeds, the rear wheels are turned in the same direction as the front. If you are parking or doing a sneaky U-turn, the back wheels steer in the opposite direction to the front. The swap-over between same-way and opposite-way steering is mechanically arranged purely on the angle of the wheels in the case of the Honda, but another 4WS car, the Mazda 626, has a speed-sensitive system.

The Japanese manufacturers built many prototypes before they got 4WS right, and the same has applied to four-wheel-drive of course. Anti-lock braking is rather a different matter because so much research and development was done by specialist manufacturers in the aircraft and automotive industry, and it still continues, as it has to be matched to progress in FWD and FWS.

TOP Way back in 1967, Jensen were trend setters with Ferguson 4WD and anti-lock disc brakes.

ABOVE The Jensen FF of 1967 had a Vignale-designed steel body, and automatic transmission.

Multiple Valves

Engine development has always been carried out separately from main prototype conception and construction, often by proprietary specialists, whilst many engine developments have derived from racing and rallying. The popularity of multiple valves – it is almost a craze – is a case in point. There is nothing new about having three or four instead of two valves per cylinder, but in recent years there has been an almost frantic search for more performance for both racing and road-going cars. Compared with supercharging (mechanical or exhaust driven) the redesigning of cylinder heads to accommodate more valves, usually in conjunction with fuel injection and overhead camshafts, is a cheaper and more reliable method of increasing volumetric efficiency and providing more power across a wide engine speed range.

Crash testing the totally successful best-selling Ford Fiesta.

Testing, Testing

Ferrari perfection, the 3.2-litre motor of 90 degree multiple-valve format.

If cars of today and tomorrow and next year move faster and faster, they must also be made to handle more safely, and this aim is conscientiously and stringently applied to prototypes and pre-production limited editions, crash tests and destruction tests being computer-simulated initially, then followed by rig tests and by track and other off-road driving.

In developing the new Fiesta, for instance, Ford used a special high-G catapult ram that can reproduce the dynamics of a severe impact non-destructively under controlled laboratory conditions. Computer-controlled slow crush rigs and steering column pendulums were also used to develop occupant protection levels to a high standard. All this was additional to the destruction of fully-equipped cars in instrumented crashes.

In designing their important new XM car, Citroen imposed severe standards for impact resistance and sound insulation. This was the first car of this marque to have its structure completely calculated prior to running the first prototype, involv-

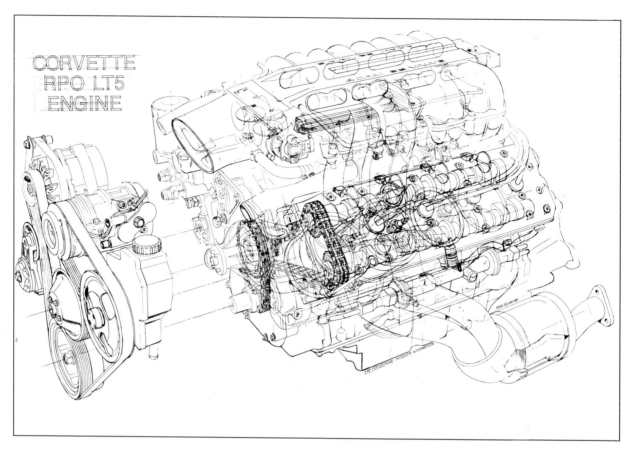

CORVETTE
RPO LT5
ENGINE

Engine of the new Chevvy Corvette ZR-1 is a joint effort
of Lotus, GM and Mercury. It is a 32-valve unit.

ing the analysis of 300 structures. The new method involved the making of a pre-prototype by calculation (the principles of structural definition phase) followed by a network model allowing the structure of the initially chosen shape to be calculated, after which the network for the definitive prototype could be arrived at.

Many prototypes and a few production cars now embody some form of what is known as active suspension, and this seems almost certain to become more generally adopted, if not universal. In essence, it uses the ubiquitous electronic control unit, or mini-computer, to monitor and adjust the suspension system instantly and constantly. Such a system is used on the new Citroen XM, whilst Lotus and Goodyear have announced a collaborative programme of development of active suspension, whereby new tyre design concepts and their testing will go hand-in-hand with the development of the springing and damping control on two European saloons provided by Goodyear and adapted by Lotus.

Constructors of prototypes fortunately have not been much, if at all, involved in dealing with emission regulations, because that has been largely a function of the specialist in engine design or the even more specialized creator of the catalysts. All that the design teams have had to do is to make room for the sometimes bulky catalysts in their body/chassis designs. Research programmes are another matter. Volkswagen spent several million pounds of their own and West German government funds in proving that lean-burn engines could not match the low pollution levels under all conditions produced by engines fitted with three-way catalysts, a costly and ultimately fruitless exercise.

Honda engineers spent a great deal of time and money on developing what they called CVCC (Compound Vortex Controlled Combustion) only to have it overtaken by increasingly demanding emission regulations so that they had to go along the same lean-burn or catalyst roads as other manufacturers.

Prototyping The Prototype

If car designers have been pathfinders in mechanical progress in body and chassis design, they have also been at pains to optimize their own functions, developing advanced systems and methods for the creation of prototypes and pre-production units. This was exemplified in the development of the new Ford Fiesta at the twin European engineering centres at Dunton in England and Merkenich in West Germany, where some 500 engineers and model makers were involved.

The team started with the creation of the body in 3 and 5-door clay models. When the style had been chosen, detailed three-dimensional surface data were taken from the approved clay model by electronic scanning bridges and recorded on digital computer tape. This master tape was then transferred to body engineering where detail information was added using graphical computers.

The surface lines generated by this process form high-precision 3-D space co-ordinates which are the key to the design of the outer skin and the manufacture of the intricate dies needed in metal stamping. The body shell was brought together in a programme of complex structural analysis work using Finite Element Methods (FEM).

FEM is presently an accepted process of stress analysis and 'structural optimization' originally developed by the aircraft industry and pioneered by Ford for car design. It represents surface forms as a complex framework of up to 30,000 reference points at which individual stresses can be calculated to create an accurate picture of a curved panel or complex pressing.

A series of simultaneous stress equations is generated from the known static, dynamic and impact loadings at the various input points such as suspension mounts or bumper attachments. By using the power of the high-speed computers, all these equations, often involving several million maths sums a second, can be solved.

From Drawing Board To Production Line

Before even the very first ideas are committed to paper, let alone given form in the model shop, engineers and designers must determine the objectives of any new project – and most importantly, analyze the principal competition. Models are made – sometimes in clay, sometimes in fibreglass – following a master draft drawing and usually *after* engineering feasibility studies.

Technical and engineering design is the last stage before
the construction of the prototype and analysis of
manufacturing feasibility. For design groups like I.DE.A,
(whose workshops are illustrated here), there may be
diversification away from auto design. They have been
involved, for example, with yachts, motorcycles, even
fashion sportswear. The principle aim does not change:
to sell something that works.

ABOVE Nissan's ceramic gas-turbine engine on display at the British Motor Show, 1985. How important will ceramics be in the future? The problem of wear resistance may prove insuperable. (Interestingly, constant attempts to manufacture a ceramic handgun have so far failed).

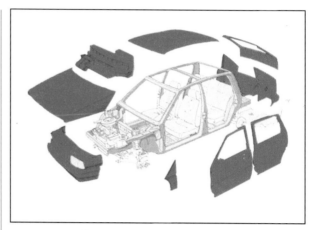

ABOVE The subsystem concept is now widespread in auto design and manufacture, whereby components are grouped according to function and treated as separate entities – here steel space frame and plastic body shell – allowing greater flexibility and decentralization of production.

These FEM techniques are also used to evaluate the detail design and critical stress levels of body joints, attachment brackets, engine mounts, door latches and hinges, etc. For the first time at Fords, the design of the interior components, mouldings and soft trim was carried out concurrently with the exterior development.

Although FEM and CAD (Computer Assisted Design) minimized early prototype work, fully engineered prototypes featuring the appearance as well as the function of the final product, were still considered essential. Each cost several thousand pounds and were built over two years ahead of launch. Hand crafting was kept minimal and as many production-type processes as possible were used.

During the later phases of component and vehicle test and development, specific homologation tests were carried out to provide formal data to the legal authorities who approve the sale of cars in each national territory.

Finally, specialist engineers from the Product Development Group continued to liaise with Manufacturing Operations Dept. on the production of tooling and the installation of vehicle assembly systems right through to the pre-production and launch phases, so as to avoid any last-minute discrepancies or problems.

New Materials

The possibilities for new materials are fascinating and bewildering. A single example is that of shape-memory alloys – metals which give signals or take action if they feel themselves getting distorted. Toyota used them in their FX-1 concept car, to control temperature in the engine compartment.

Much work is being done in developing ceramics that will stand up to high temperatures and stresses and wear-resistance and Toyota have already used them in diesel engine pre-combustion chambers, whilst ceramic pistons may not be so far off. Fibre-reinforcing of metals used in engine construction appears to have an important future.

There will be continued and possibly dramatic research into the subject of alternative fuels, including the fuel cell, whilst solar power finds a niche in the archives and technological dossiers of several manufacturing groups. Some people think there may be a comeback for the gas turbine. Certainly the case is not closed.

Many concept cars are test beds for information systems. Driver information is an area in which rapid strides are being made: for example, large fascia display units combining video, compact disc, car phone, etc. plus a dozen information channels for visual display of driver information, fuel consumption, air conditioning patterns, average speed, disfunction warnings etc. The system could be hooked up to an outside information centre for weather and route information. Car-to-centre and car-to-car communication is bound to be extended, although automatic routeing is still very far ahead, and automatic inter-car distancing by radar or other means is still very much in its infancy.

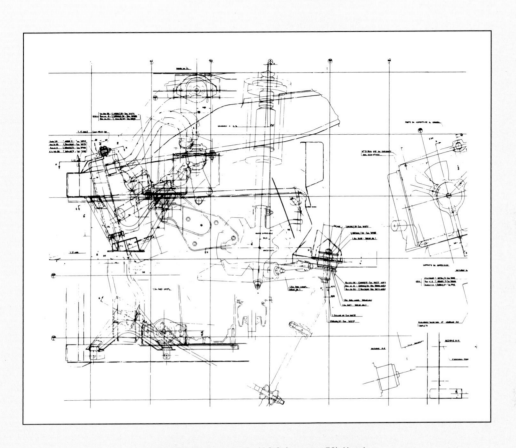

Technical drawing for the V.S.S. (see page 72). How is
the work of an auto designer to be defined? His creations
must appeal aesthetically, but they must also involve
precision engineering. This drawing – and thousands of
others like it – is not only mystifying to the non-specialist
driving his or her Fiat along the Autostrada, it is also
fascinating, and, in its own way, beautiful. The most
successful prototypes are products of science and
aesthetics: and the people who create them must be
masters of both.

INDEX

All illustrations in this book are from the J Baker Collection, from manufacturers' archives, or from the author's own collection. The author and publishers would like to thank all manufacturers for their patient cooperation in supplying images and information.